MUSICAL FORM

AMS PRESS
NEW YORK

AUGENER'S EDITION No. 9187.

MUSICAL FORM

BY

EBENEZER PROUT

B.A. Lond.

*(Hon. Mus. Doc. Trin. Coll. Dublin and Edinburgh, and
Professor of Music in the University of Dublin.)*

NINTH IMPRESSION

AUGENER Ltd.

LONDON

MT
58
.P85
1971

Reprinted from the edition of 1893, London
First AMS EDITION published 1971
Manufactured in the United States of America

International Standard Book Number: 0-404-05145-6

Library of Congress Catalog Number: 70-137280

AMS PRESS INC.
NEW YORK, N.Y. 10003

PREFACE.

THE preceding volumes of this series have dealt chiefly with matters of musical theory, though theory and practice are so closely connected that it is impossible to draw a hard and fast line of demarcation between them. The present volume, on the other hand, is almost entirely practical, and points of theory are hardly touched upon.

None of the earlier works of the series have involved anything like the amount of labour in their preparation that has been needful for this one. Very little is to be found in English musical literature concerning the subjects which occupy the greater part of the volume; and the materials had to be compiled partly from large German treatises on composition, which, however interesting and instructive, can certainly not be considered as "light reading," and, to a still larger extent, from the careful and often minute analysis of the works of the great masters. This, it is hoped, will be deemed a sufficient apology for the delay in the appearance of the present volume.

In dealing with the subject of Musical Form, the author felt that the only satisfactory and logical method was to begin with the rudiments. Rhythm—that is, the more or less regular recurrence of cadence, is as much an essential of music as it is of poetry. The first part of this volume is therefore devoted to an examination of the fundamental principles of Rhythm, as shown in the construction of musical phrases and sentences. Such an examination would have been incomplete without the analysis of a musical sentence into its ultimate constituents—the *motives* In his treatment of this part of the subject the author must express his deep indebtedness to the researches of Dr. Hugo Riemann. He believes that this distinguished German theorist has been the first to recognize fully the true nature of the motive, and the connection of its unaccented notes, not with the preceding, but with the following accented note. With this view.

which is fully explained in the third chapter of the present volume, the author most emphatically agrees ; and its comprehension and acknowledgment make clear many things in the works of the great composers which otherwise appear incorrect, or at least difficult of justification (see, for instance, the passages quoted in §§ 64, 65). While differing in many details from Dr. Riemann as to its application, the author believes the principle itself to be of such importance that it is hardly too much to say that the whole teaching of this volume stands or falls by the acceptance or rejection of the views here set forth as to the nature of the motive.

To the analytical method followed up to this point succeeds the synthetical. Having divided sentences into motives, the next thing is to build up motives into sentences. But, inasmuch as many sentences contain modulations, it was first necessary to go fully into the whole question of key-relationship and modulation. These matters had been partially treated in Chapter IX. of *Harmony* (which, however, dealt only with nearly related keys), and, incidentally in later chapters of the same book. The author felt that a more systematic and thorough investigation of the subject was desirable here ; and three chapters of this volume are therefore devoted to its consideration. While it was evidently impossible to explain or classify every *possible* modulation—for it cannot be said that the possibilities are even yet exhausted—it is hoped that the student will find in these chapters sufficient guidance for all practical purposes.

Only those who have investigated the subject will have any idea how much variety is possible in the construction of a simple sentence of the regular rhythm of eight bars. The different forms of the eight-bar sentence are treated of in Chapter VII., and illustrated by a large number of examples from the works of the great composers. To these are added sentences of twelve and sixteen bars—that is to say, such as contain three or four four-bar phrases, instead of only two. These may be regarded as extensions of the normal sentence ; but it seemed more suitable to include them in this chapter than to class them among the irregular rhythms.

The construction of phrases and sentences of other than the normal length, though often incidentally referred to in other books, has not, so far as the author is aware, been systematically treated and fully accounted for in any book in our language.

One of the longest chapters in the present volume is therefore devoted to this subject, the difficulties of which, it is believed, are more apparent than real. It is hoped that the explanations here given will smooth the path of the student of analysis, and will also indicate to the young composer the principles which must guide him in ascertaining whether any sentence of irregular length which he may have written be correct or not. For the excellent and clear method of indicating the nature of these irregular rhythms by means of figures placed under the bars, the author is again indebted to Dr. Riemann.

The last two chapters of the present volume treat of the two typical forms—the Binary and the Ternary—out of which all others are developed. Hardly two authorities are in exact agreement as to the definition of these two forms; and the author dares not venture to hope that the lines here laid down will be universally accepted as correct. But the plan adopted in these chapters has at least the advantage of being intelligible and consistent, and is the result of much thought, and of a careful examination of a large number of movements by the great composers. It was found impossible to establish a clear line of demarcation between the two forms, except by considering the Ternary as an extension, and not a variation, of the Binary.

An explanation may perhaps be desirable of the reasons why no fewer than nine complete movements, some of which are very familiar, are given in full in the last chapter of this book. In the first place, it was felt that, if the movements in question were only referred to, many readers would either not have them in their libraries, or would not have them at hand for reference; and even of those who had the music, it is probable that many would not take the trouble to take it down from the bookcase and refer to it. But the principal reason was, that, by giving the pieces entire, an opportunity was afforded, such as otherwise would have been quite impossible, of practically illustrating the principles laid down in Chapter VIII. as to the construction of sentences of irregular length. Every one of these nine pieces is furnished with a complete rhythmical analysis of all its sentences; and the student who will take the trouble to follow these analyses carefully will find comparatively little difficulty in analyzing for himself any compositions which he may be studying. No perfection is claimed for the analyses here given; very often more than one division into phrases, &c., is possible; but the methods described in the eighth chapter have been systematically adhered to; and the results will at least be found to be intelligible and consistent.

As the present work treats chiefly of the fundamental principles of form, the practical application of these principles, as we find them in the larger works of the great masters (symphonies, quartetts, sonatas, &c.), does not come within the scope of this volume. This will be dealt with in the next volume of this series, which will be devoted to what are generally known as *Applied Forms*.

The author had nearly completed the present book when he had his attention directed to the late Rudolf Westphal's 'Allgemeine Theorie der Musikalischen Rhythmik, seit J. S. Bach' ('General Theory of Musical Rhythm, since J. S. Bach'). This most valuable and interesting work, the author of which was Professor of Greek at Moscow University, shows that the principles of rhythm, as understood by the Greeks, and set forth in the treatise of Aristoxenus (300 B.C.), a pupil of Aristotle, are in all essentials the same which guided Bach and Beethoven in their compositions. It was with no small satisfaction that the author found, on reading Westphal's book, that the principles there enunciated were in every important respect the same that are set forth in the present volume. He is thereby strengthened in his belief that the views here enunciated. are sound, and that the general principles of art are immutable from one age to another.

The author has already acknowledged his obligations to Dr. Riemann's works for many of the more important features of the present volume. Whatever originality (if any) there may be in the work is rather in the way in which the ideas are presented than in the ideas themselves. He has collected his material from whatever sources were accessible to him, and, besides Dr. Riemann's 'Musikalische Dynamik und Agogik,' 'Katechismus der Compositionslehre,' and 'Katechismus der Phrasirung,' he must express his indebtedness to Marx's 'Compositionslehre,' and, to some extent, to Bussler and Cornell's 'Theory and Practice of Musical Form.' He has also once more to thank his friend Dr. C. W. Pearce for his kindness in revising the proof-sheets of the volume.

LONDON, *May*, 1893.

NOTE.

The references throughout this volume, to "Harmony: Its Theory and Practice," refer to the Revised Edition.

For the convenience of those who may desire to continue to use copies of the First to the Fifteenth Editions, inclusive, the following table is inserted :—

Revised Edition.	First to Fifteenth Editions.	Revised Edition	First to Fifteenth Editions.
Chapter II	Chapter III	Section 228	Section 192
" III	" IV	" 239	" 202
" IX	" X	" 251	" 207
" X	" XI	" 258	" 211
" XI	" XIX	" 294	" 243
" XVI	" XVIII	" 307	" 248
		" 313–321	" 253–258
		" 314	" 254
		" 318	" 257
Section 75	Section 103	" 325	" 263
" 77	" 105	" 336	" 504
" 93–95	" 126–128	" 341	" 517
" 104	" 113	" 411	" 381
" 133	" 137	" 418	" 75
" 169	" 156	" 428	" 410
" 173	" 159	" 433	" 404
" 188–189	" 164–166	" 440	" 432
		" 490, 491, 505, 507, 520	" 426 (a) (b) 433, 439 & 460 (d)
" 208	" 170–171		
" 224	" 190	" 645–647	" 562, 564

TABLE OF CONTENTS.

[*N.B.—The numbers refer in every instance to the sections, not to the pages.*]

CHAPTER I.—INTRODUCTION ... ... *page* 1

The construction of works of art, 1—Definition of *Form*, 2—A work without form, 3—The Fantasia, 4—The essentials of Form, 5—Melody, 6—Tonality, 7 —Cadence and Rhythm, 8, 9—Proportion, 10—Modulation, 11—Development, 12—The connection of Melody and Harmony, 13, 14—Melodic invention cannot be taught, 15—The best models of form, 16.

CHAPTER II.—RHYTHM—SENTENCES AND PHRASES... ... ... *page* 6

Analogy between music and poetry, 18—The distinction between poetry and prose; regularity of accent, 19, 20—Varieties of verse, 21—Music resembles verse, not prose, 22—Rhythm a question of the position of cadences, 23—A *Sentence*, or *Period* defined, 24—The most usual lengths of a sentence, 25—Reason for the prevalence of two-, four-, or eight-bar rhythm, 26—A *Phrase* defined, 27— Sentence in a minor key ; the " feminine ending," 28—The first phrase ending with a middle cadence, 29, 30—Ditto with a full cadence, 31—Modulation in the first phrase, 32, 33—Modulation at the end of a sentence, 34, 35—Quadruple time is really *compound* time, 36—Music in quadruple time often inaccurately barred, 37—Accented and unaccented bars, 38—How to determine which bars are accented, 39—Example by Beethoven, 40—Other examples referred to, 41—Sentences containing three phrases, 42, 43—Sentences of four phrases ; example by Haydn, 44—Ditto by Mozart ; overlapping of phrases, 45 —Ditto by Mendelssohn ; two phrases of four bars answered by one of eight, 46 —Ditto by Wagner, 47.

CHAPTER III.—THE SUBDIVISIONS OF A MUSICAL SENTENCE—SECTIONS AND MOTIVES... ... ... *page* 23

Phrases subdivisible, 49—" Fore-phrase " and "after-phrase "; their relation to one another, 50—The *Section ;* how to find its limits, 51, 52—Some phrases not divisible into sections, 53—The harmony to be considered in making subdivisions, 54—Slighter cadential effect usual in sections, 55—An exception, 56— The *Motive*, the germ from which music is developed, 58—The general principle regulating the form of the motive, 59—Phrases beginning with an incomplete motive, 60—A sentence divided into motives, 61—A less simple sentence analyzed, 62—The feminine ending, 63—When it is to be assumed ; importance of correct division into motives in explaining harmonic progressions, 64, 65— The motives correspond to the *words* of a sentence, 66—Example by Haydn, 67 —Sub-motives, 68—The motive defined, 69—Motives of two bars, 70, 71— Motives with feminine endings, 72—The constituents of a motive, 73— Summary of the whole question, 74—The principles only apply fully to sentences of regular construction, 75.

CHAPTER IV.—MODULATION—KEY-RELATIONSHIP...   ...   ...   *page* 37

Modulation defined; "transient" modulation, 77—Use of the motive in determining the point of modulation, 78, 79—Key-relationship; nearly related keys, 80—Degrees of nearness in relationship of major keys, 81—Ditto in minor keys, 82—Keys in the second degree of relationship, 83—Chords common to such keys, 84, 85—Chords in which an enharmonic change is implied, 86—Minor keys related in the second degree to a major key, 87—Keys in the second degree of relationship to a minor key, 88–90—The minor key the converse of the major, 91—Unrelated keys, 92, 93—Table of Related Keys, 94.

CHAPTER V.—THE MEANS OF MODULATION—MODULATION BY MEANS
     OF TRIADS   ...   .   *page* 44

The means of modulation almost exhaustless, 95—Modulation by chords common to two keys; example by Mozart, 96-99—Modulations in minor keys; example by Beethoven, 100—Ditto by Bach, 101—Modulation by triads, 102—Modulations by a major triad which is diatonic in both keys, 103-106—Such modulations require to be confirmed, 107—Diatonic minor triads, 108—Possible modulations with these, 109—Modulation with more than one ambiguous chord, 110—Modulation to an unrelated key, 111—Modulation by means of chromatic triads, 112, 113—Examples of extreme modulations, 114—Modulations between keys in the second degree of relationship, 115—Modulation to the mediant major, 116—Suggestions of related minor keys, 117—Modulation to the flat submediant, 118—Ditto to the submediant and flat mediant, 119—Example of modulation between keys in the second degree of relationship, by Mozart, 120—Ditto by Beethoven, 121—Ditto by Schubert, 122—Ditto by Brahms, 123—Modulations between unrelated keys; example by Beethoven, 124.—Ditto by Schubert, 125, 126—Ditto by Dvořák, 127.

CHAPTER VI.—THE MEANS OF MODULATION (*continued*) ...   ...   *page* 57

Modulation by means of fundamental discords, 130—The fundamental sevenths; example by Wagner, 131—Modulation by means of the diminished triad, 132—The diatonic sevenths; which forms are available for modulation, 133—Examples by Bach, 134, 135—Ditto by Mendelssohn, 136, ;137—Modulation by chromatic chords of the major ninth, 138—*Enharmonic modulation*, 139—Ditto by chords of the minor ninth; example by Mozart, 140—Ditto by Handel, 141—Ditto by Spohr, 142—Ditto by Beethoven, 143—The enharmonic change of fundamental sevenths to augmented sixths, 144—Examples by Schubert, 145-148—Ditto by Beethoven, 149, 150—The enharmonic changes of the dominant minor thirteenth, 151—Examples, 152, 153—Modulations without a connecting chord, 154—An implied enharmonic modulation *possible*, 155—One note of a chord retained in the following chord, 156—Modulation by means of scale passages, 157, 158—*Compound modulation;* example by Schubert, 159—The exact point of modulation, 160—Less frequent methods of modulating; example by Mozart, 161, 162—Ditto by Schubert, 163, 164—Ditto by Wagner, 165, 166—Analysis of chromatic modulations, 167—No definite rules as to choice of modulations can be given, 168—Exercises in modulating, 169.

CHAPTER VII. — THE CONSTRUCTION OF SIMPLE SENTENCES WITH
     REGULAR RHYTHM ...   ., ...   *page* 78

Modulation in short sentences, 170—What to do with the motive, 171—The typical motive, 172—Its repetition at a different pitch, 173—Varying the lengths of the notes, 174—Inversion, 175—Augmentation and diminution, 176—

Sentences constructed from the typical motive, 177—Example by Beethoven, 178
—Alteration of interval, 179—The "rhythmical figure," 180—Disguised
motives, 181, 182—Contrasted motives, 183—Construction of eight-bar sentences, 184—The accented bars, 185—Cadences of the fore-phrase, 186—Construction of the sections, 187—Formula for indicating the subdivisions of sentences, 188—Various forms of the eight-bar sentence, 189–193—Ditto with
modulations, 194–198—Modulation to an unrelated key ; example by Schubert,
199—A complete composition only eight bars in length, 200—The formulæ for
eight-bar sentences in which only one phrase is divided into sections, 201—
Models of such sentences, 202–205—Method of composition, 206—Formulæ
for sentences in which both phrases are divided into sections, 207—Where to
change the harmony, 208—Effect of the anticipation of the harmony on an
unaccented beat or bar, 209—Twelve-bar sentences, 210—Similarity of
phrases, 211, 212—Repetition of cadence, 213—Repetition of the second
phrase, 214—Twelve-bar sentences mostly the extensions of eight-bar, 215—
Sixteen-bar sentences, 216—Example by Mozart, 217—Ditto by Mendelssohn,
analyzed, 219—The *normal* form of sentence, where mostly to be met
with, 220.

CHAPTER VIII.—IRREGULAR AND COMPLEX RHYTHMS ... ... *page* 102

Irregular rhythms are variations of the normal rhythm, not new forms, 221—Prolongations of the final cadence, 222—Lengthening the last notes of the cadence,
223—Repetition and prolongation, 224—Method of indicating such repetitions,
225—Extension of cadence, 227—Repetition of ditto with variation, 228—
Cadential prolongation in both the phrases of a sentence, 229—Other methods
of extending the end of a sentence, 230, 231—Prolongation of the beginning
of a sentence, 232—Repetition of a section in the middle of a sentence, 233—
A sentence greatly prolonged, 234–236—Such prolongations result from the
composer's musical feeling, 237—Lengthening of a phrase by the interpolation
of an unaccented bar ; example by Mozart, 238—Ditto by Mendelssohn, 239—
Ditto by Schubert ; *five-bar rhythm*, 240—The interpolation of an unaccented
bar mostly takes place in approaching a cadence, 241—Interpolation of an
accented bar, 242, 243—The interpolated bar repeated sequentially ; example by
Beethoven, 244—Accented bars inserted in both phrases of a sentence, 245, 246
—The difference of effect produced by the interpolation of unaccented and accented bars, 247—Contraction of a sentence; elision of an unaccented bar, 248
—Effect of elision of the first bar of a sentence, 249—Example, an Anglican
chant, 250—Elision of an intermediate unaccented bar ; examples by Mendel-
ssohn, 251, 252—How to distinguish between elision of an unaccented, and in-
terpolation of an accented bar, 253—*Three-bar rhythm*, 254—Examples in
national music, 255—Reason of the satisfactory effect of three-bar rhythm, 256
—Beethoven's '*ritmo di tre battute*' in the ninth symphony, explained, 257
—The overlapping of two phrases or sentences, 258—Example by Dussek, 259
—Ditto by Schumann, 260—Ditto by Mendelssohn, 261—*seven-bar rhythm*,
Example by Beethoven, 262, 263—Ditto by Mozart, 264—Establishing a figure
of accompaniment, 265—Beginning in the middle of a sentence, 266, 267—
Elision of an entire unaccented phrase, 268—The complex rhythms of polyphonic music, 269—Analysis of a fugue by Bach, 270–276—In fugues regularity
of accent often supplies the place of regular rhythm, 277—The reason for this,
278—Analysis of passages containing irregular rhythms ; example by Haydn
279, 280—Ditto by Schubert, 281, 282—Ditto by Mozart (three bar rhythm),
283, 284—Ditto by Haydn, 285—When are deviations from regular rhythm
most suitable, 286—*Cross-accents ;* examples by Beethoven, 287, 288—Ditto by
Weber, 289, 290—Curious example by Schumann, 291—Example by Clementi,
292—Effect of augmentation produced by cross-accents, 293—The insertion of
one beat in a bar ; example by Handel, 295—Ditto by Schumann, 296—Ditto
by Mendelssohn, 297—Change in the subdivision of the bar, 298—The elision
of a single beat, 299—*Quintuple time ;* example by Handel, 300—Ditto by
Boieldieu, 301—Ditto by Chopin, 302—*Septuple time ;* example by Liszt, 303—
Ditto by Berlioz, 304—Hints to the student, 305.

CHAPTER IX.—The Simple Binary Form ...   . *page* 151

Binary Form defined, 306—The development of the larger forms from the smaller, 307—The simplest binary forms; hymn-tunes and double chants, 308, 309—The concise binary form of two sentences; examples by Schumann, 310–312—Ditto by Corelli, 313—Minuet and Trio, by Mozart, 314—Example by Schubert, 315—Ditto by Haydn, 316—Ditto by Beethoven, 317—Use of this form in vocal music, 318—Example by Weber, 319—Ditto by Mozart, 320—The binary form with sentences of less regular length, 321—Example by Haydn, analyzed, 322—Analysis of Gavotte by Bach, 323–325—Ditto of Minuet by Handel, 326—Irregular rhythms illustrated, 327—The extended binary form in vocal music; example by Handel, 328, 329—The binary form with two subjects, 330—Analysis of Prelude by Bach, 331, 332—Adagio by Mozart analyzed, 333–335—Importance of this variety of binary form, 336—The name "two-part Song-Form" as applied to Binary Form, 337—Hints for first attempts in composition, 338—Writing hymn-tunes, 339, 340—Outlines to be filled up, 341, 342—Original tunes, 343—Paraphrasing given examples, 344 —Short pieces with two and three sentences, 345—Ditto with four sentences; variety of cadence and order of modulation, 346—Hints for the construction of sentences of irregular length, 347.

CHAPTER X.—The Simple Ternary Form   ...   . *page* 184

Definition of *Ternary Form*, 348—Different views of theorists, 349—*Episode* an essential of ternary form, 350—Example by Mozart, referred to, 351—The first part of a ternary movement must be a complete binary form, 352—The principal theme must recur in the third part, 353—The elasticity of this form, 354 —Analysis of the andante of Beethoven's sonata, Op. 79, 355, 356—Andante by Mozart analyzed, 357, 358—Ditto by Haydn, 359–361—Analysis of the Adagio of the 'Sonata Pathètique,' 362–369—Ditto of the Adagio of Beethoven's sonata, Op. 31, No. 1, 370–373—Ditto of the Adagio of Weber's sonata in C, 374–377—The ternary form rarely used in large works except for slow movements or minuets, 378—Use of the ternary as an independent form, 379 — Example by Chopin, 380, 381 — Ditto by Schubert, 382–383 — Ditto by Schumann, 386–391—The ternary form in vocal music, 392—Air by Handel analyzed, 393—Examples referred to, 394—A "mixed form," 395, 396—Modern examples of ternary form in vocal music, 397—The middle portion may be in different tempo, 398, 399—General summary, 400—All larger forms are developed from the typical binary or ternary form—Conclusion, 401.

MUSICAL FORM.

—◆—

CHAPTER I.

INTRODUCTION.

1. **Every** work of art, whether of small or large dimensions, must be constructed in accordance with some definitely formed plan in the mind of the artist. We cannot conceive of a painter going to his easel and beginning to work on his canvas without having decided what was to be the subject of his picture. Nobody but a lunatic would set to work before he had made up his mind whether he was going to paint a bit of 'still life,' a portrait, a landscape, or a piece of architecture. The details of his picture might, and most probably would, undergo more or less important modifications during the progress of his work; but its general design would be clearly in his mind before he began operations. Similarly, an architect would know perfectly well whether he were going to design a private dwelling-house, a shop, a church, or a concert-hall; and he would lay out his plans according to the kind of building required.

2. A composer goes to work on the same principle. Before putting pen to paper, he makes up his mind what sort of piece he is going to write. Nobody in the world ever sat down to write a set of waltzes, and found, when he had finished, that he had composed a fugue instead. The simple reason is, that the two works are constructed on an entirely different plan. The plan, or design according to which a piece of music is written, is called its FORM.

3. It is rather difficult to imagine a composer sitting down to write without any definite idea of what he was going to compose. Let us try for a moment to think what would be the probable result. Assuming him to be naturally gifted, and that his ideas flowed freely, his thoughts would ramble on in an aimless manner, without logical connexion; and the whole piece would be a mere incoherent rhapsody of the nature of an improvisation. If he had no ability, the result would be a musical chaos—"without form and void." But to a talented musician, such a thing as **we**

are supposing would be almost impossible. Just as, when we are thinking, one thought naturally suggests the next one, so to the musician there would be an involuntary connexion of ideas, more or less clearly recognizable, and an absolutely incoherent piece by a good composer is hardly conceivable

4. Almost the only kind of composition without a clearly defined form is the *Fantasia,*—a piece in which (as its name implies) the composer is left free to follow his own fantasy. But if we examine the different examples of the Fantasia left us by the great composers—Haydn, Mozart, Beethoven, Mendelssohn, or Schumann—we shall find in all of them clear evidences of design, though the plan of the different pieces varies too much to allow us to make any generalizations as to the form of a Fantasia.

5. It was said just now that by the *Form* of a piece of music is meant the plan on which it is constructed. These words, however, without further explanation will convey but a vague impression to the student, who may not unnaturall) ask what there is to plan. The object of the present volume is to answer this question as far as possible; and our first enquiry will be, What are the constituents of that which is called Musical Form? Expressed in the fewest possible words, they may be said to be Melody, Tonality, Rhythm, and Proportion. To these in all larger works, and in most smaller, must be added Modulation and Development.

6. The simplest definition of Melody is perhaps the following— " If sounds of different pitch are heard one after the other we get MELODY " (*Harmony,* § 3 *). This definition, however, by itself is quite inadequate; for it is possible to write a succession of sounds which by no conceivable stretch of imagination can be called a melody, as for example the following—

It is clear therefore that something more than mere difference of pitch enters into the composition of melody.

7. The student will hardly require to be told that the series of notes just given can in no sense be regarded as a melody, because it is in no *key.* Here therefore the second of our constituents of Form, viz: TONALITY, comes into requisition. Without a clearly defined tonality, music is impossible. But even tonality by itself is not sufficient to make a series of different notes into a satisfactory melody. We will write such a series in the key of C, and will, moreover, write it in common time, marking the position of the accents by bars.

* The references to *Harmony, Counterpoint, &c,* throughout this work refer in all cases to the other volumes of this series.   (Augener Ltd.)

This is at all events more intelligible than the atrocious series of intervals given in the last section; but it still fails to satisfy either the ear or the mind. Why is this? What is it that is still wanting?

8. The best way to answer this question will be to rewrite the above bars, making such modifications as are necessary to render the succession of sounds satisfying to the ear. Only very slight alterations will be required :—

It will be seen that the only changes made have been the extending of the seventh bar into two, with a point of repose at the eighth bar, and the addition of the tonic at the end. Though commonplace enough, and of the least possible value in itself, we have now an intelligible and satisfactory melody, which before we had not.

9. Those who have studied the harmonizing of melodies (*Counterpoint*, Ch. XVI.) will see that in the above musical sentence two *Cadences* have been introduced—a half cadence (*Counterpoint*, § 506) at the eighth bar, and a full cadence (*Counterpoint*, § 482) at the sixteenth bar. These cadences divide the music into two equal parts of eight bars each; it is therefore said to be in "eight-bar RHYTHM." The whole question of the nature and functions of Rhythm will be discussed in the next chapter; it will be sufficient here to say that by the word 'Rhythm' is meant the more or less regular recurrence of cadences. A comparison of the two passages in §§ 7, 8 will show what an important part it plays in even the simplest music; it may indeed be said that Melody and Rhythm are inseparable.

10. We will now once more alter the melody given in § 8.

We have entirely spoilt the music by this last alteration, though we have still the same two cadences as before. The utterly unsatisfactory effect of this new version arises from the fact that the cadences now divide the music quite irregularly, the first strain (or "phrase") containing five bars, and the second nine. This illustrates the fourth of the essentials of Form mentioned in § 5—the necessity of PROPORTION. The two parts of the melody are badly balanced. The student must not infer that it is necessary that the cadences should always recur at exactly the same distances. In smaller compositions, especially in dance-music, this is often the case; but if a larger work, such as a symphony or sonata, were cut up by cadences into regular sections of four or eight bars throughout (just as a linendraper might measure and cut off tape by the yard), the effect would be monotonous in the extreme. Nevertheless, as we shall see later, there must be some kind of balance, some proportion between the various subdivisions of a piece of music.

11. In all except the smallest and simplest forms, MODULATION plays an important part. It is, however, not so absolutely essential as the points we have already touched on, as it is possible to compose short pieces, the form of which shall be quite satisfactory, and yet which contain no modulations at all. Many well-known double chants are examples of this.

12. Another important constituent of most larger forms is DEVELOPMENT. By this is meant the treatment of a theme, often composed of only a few notes, by the various devices—sequential imitation, inversion, augmentation, diminution, &c.—at the command of the composer, in such a way as to obtain unity in the whole; that is to say that there shall be logical connexion between the various parts of the work. The instrumental works of the great composers are full of these developments. In very small pieces there is often no opportunity for them, though even among these, specimens are to be found, as we shall see later, which have been developed from an apparently insignificant germ.

13. It must never be forgotten that there is a very intimate relation between melody and harmony. So much is this the case, that it is almost impossible for a musician to compose a melody without an implied harmonic groundwork. Hence the frequent use of melodic passages which are simply chords broken, or taken in arpeggio, as in the following commencement of a well-known Welsh air—

It will be seen that the first two bars consist of notes of the tonic chord, the third bar of the supertonic, the fourth bar of the dominant, and so on. The melody itself irresistibly *suggests* its own harmony, and this would be none the less the case were passing notes introduced between the different notes of the chords.

14. A similar point is illustrated by the following melody—

Mozart. ' Figaro.

Let the student play or sing this melody without any harmony, and observe how evidently it is founded upon the harmonies with which the composer has accompanied it, and of which we have given only the basses.

15. It must here be distinctly said that no attempt will be made in this book to teach the *invention* of melody. The only thing possible here is to teach its construction. Like a poet, a composer is born, not made. Education is as necessary in the one case as in the other; and just as a poet could produce nothing of value without having studied the laws of grammar and prosody, so the musician must devote himself to the study of theory, if he would attain excellence. Harmony and Counterpoint are his grammar; Form is his prosody. Moreover, just as one may have a perfect knowledge both of grammar and prosody, and yet be no poet, a musician may have a thorough knowledge of theory, and yet be no composer. Melody is a gift from Heaven, the invention of which cannot possibly be taught; our object is to show the student how to make the best use of the gifts that Heaven may have bestowed upon him; anything more is out of our power.

16. The best models of form are to be found in what is known as "absolute" music, that is, instrumental music not written on any definite programme. If a composer is endeavouring to illustrate any special subject, the nature of his subject will probably modify the form of the work. The same is often the case with vocal music, in which the words exercise an important influence on the form, especially in dramatic music.

17. We shall now proceed to the study of the various forms, beginning with the simplest; but it will first be necessary to deal at some length with the important question of Rhythm.

B

CHAPTER II.

RHYTHM—SENTENCES AND PHRASES.

18 There is considerable analogy between the construction of music and of poetry; and it will be of much assistance to the student in endeavouring to understand the subject of Rhythm, with which we are now about to deal, if we illustrate it by reference to the sister art.

19. Everybody knows that what distinguishes poetry from prose, so far as its form is concerned, is, that in poetry the accents, and to a less extent the cadences of the verse, recur at more or less regular intervals, while in prose they do not do so. Let us, as an illustration, take some familiar lines, the commencement of Longfellow's ' Excelsior '—

> " The shades of night were falling fast,
> As through an Alpine village passed
> A youth, who bore, 'mid snow and ice,
> A banner with a strange device,
> Excelsior ! "

Everyone who reads these verses feels that the accent recurs regularly on every second syllable, and that after every eighth syllable there is a cadence marking the end of a line,* each line therefore containing four accents. The last line, which has only four syllables, is a kind of " coda " to the stanza.

20. In the passage we have just quoted the cadential feeling is strengthened by the rhymes at the end of the lines; but that rhyme is by no means a necessity in poetry, and that the cadences can be quite clearly felt without its aid, will be seen by another short extract—from Longfellow's ' Song of Hiawatha '—

> " Round and round they wheeled and darted,
> Filled the Evening Star with music,
> With their songs of joy and freedom ;
> Filled the Evening Star with splendour,
> With the fluttering of their plumage. "

Here the cadential feeling is just as distinct as in the ' Excelsior '; each line again contains four accents, and the accents come on every second syllable. It is the combined regularity of accent and, in a less degree, of cadence that makes the above passage verse, and not prose.

21. We have just said "and *in a less degree* of cadence." It is hardly needful to remind the student that it is by no means

---

* The word "verse" would be perhaps more accurate than "line" here; but, as confusion might arise from the fact that "verse" is so often used as equivalent to " stanza " (*e.g.*, "a hymn of four *verses* "), we prefer to retain the more common expression.

necessary that all the lines of a poem should be of the same
length. It would be superfluous to quote examples of lines of
different lengths ; they are to be met with everywhere. Neither
do the accents always occur on every second syllable. Often we
find them on every third syllable, as in the line—

" The Assyrian came down like the wolf on the fold."

The portion contained between one accent and the next is termed
by prosodists a *Foot.* Sometimes feet of two and three syllables
are combined in the same line, as in Tennyson's

" But the tender grace of a day that is dead
Will never come back to me."

What is really needed is, that there shall be some kind of system
in the placing of the accents and cadences, but not that there
shall be absolute uniformity.

22. All music, even the simplest, resembles poetry in requiring
regularity of accent and system in cadence. With regard to the
former, there is greater strictness in music than in verse ; for, with
very rare exceptions, the accents recur at perfectly regular distances throughout a piece of music. The only analogy in music
to prose is to be found in recitative, which is simply declamation
sung instead of spoken ; and in the Gregorian intonation, and the
" reciting notes ' of the chants to which the psalms are often
sung in our churches.

23. After what has been said, the student will be in a position
to understand the analogy we have spoken of between poetry and
music. In what is to follow we assume his thorough familiarity
with the whole subject of cadences. If his ideas on this matter
are at all misty, we advise him to read Chapters XV. and XVI. of
Counterpoint, to refresh his memory. As Rhythm is entirely a
question of the position of the cadences, it is evident that unless
these are thoroughly understood further progress is impossible.

24. As our first example we will take the commencement of a
well-known choral—

Choral : " O gesegnetes Regieren. '

Va   Ia

We have already used this passage in *Counterpoint* (§ 512), as an
illustration of simple forms of cadence, and we now employ it to
show the most common variety of rhythm. It will be seen that
the passage contains eight bars, and that there is a half-cadence at
the fourth bar and a full cadence at the end.* A passage ending
with a cadence, and which can be subdivided by some form
of middle cadence into at least two parts, is called a SENTENCE or
PERIOD.

* The figures under the notes (V*a*, I*a*, &c.) in this and the following examples
indicate the harmonies of the last notes of the cadences.

25. If we analyze this sentence, we see that it naturally divides itself into two equal parts, the division being marked by the half-cadence, and each half containing four accents. Each of these halves therefore corresponds in this respect to the verses by Long-fellow that we quoted above. In an enormous majority of musical periods the number of accents, and therefore of bars, consists of some multiple of 2,—either 4, 8, or even 16 bars. We shall see later that sentences can also be constructed of other lengths than these ; but such are exceptional.

26. The cause of the extreme prevalence of two-, four-, or eight-bar rhythm, as compared with any other, is the natural feeling for balance of one part against the other. Of this the student can convince himself by a very simple experiment. Let him listen to any sound repeated at regular intervals, such as the ticking of a clock or the pulsations of a locomotive steam-engine. He will find himself involuntarily counting them in twos and fours. He cannot, without a mental effort, think of them as falling in groups of three ; and after trying to feel them in threes for a while, as soon as his attention relaxes, they will fall into twos again of themselves. We cannot help feeling one tick of the clock as accented and the next as unaccented, though, as a matter of fact, they may be both of exactly the same strength. And what is true of the ticking of a clock also applies to musical forms. After a statement (*Thesis*) we require a corresponding reply (*Antithesis*), just as the shortest poem must contain at least two lines. Let the student compare the two melodies given in the last chapter in §§ 8 and 10, and note how perfectly satisfactory is the effect of the first, because eight bars are answered by eight, while the very reverse is the case with the second, because five bars are answered by nine. No isolated phrase, even though ending with a full cadence, can make a *sentence*, because the want of a response creates a feeling of incompleteness. The following passage illustrates this—

ARNE. 'Artaxerxes.'

Here, in spite of the full cadence at the end, the mind clearly feels the want of something to follow. One phrase by itself is as incomplete as half a pair of scissors.

27. We now give another example of an eight-bar sentence—this time in triple instead of in common time—

HAYDN. Symphony in C.

Except that the accents come on every third instead of on every
second beat, and that it commences on an unaccented instead of
an accented note, this sentence is precisely similar in its construction to that given in § 24. It has a half cadence at the
fourth bar, and a full cadence at the eighth. The two passages
of four bars each into which the sentence is divided by the middle
cadence are called PHRASES. The first subdivision of a sentence
will invariably be into phrases. Such short sentences as we have
given generally contain two phrases ; in longer sentences we not
infrequently find a larger number. Such sentences will be spoken
of later.

28. The following passage shows the same construction of a
sentence in a minor key—

Here again we have a half cadence ending the first phrase, at the
fifth quaver of the fourth bar. We see here also an example
of what is termed by prosodists a "feminine ending"—that is,
the ending of a verse (in musical language, of a "phrase") on an
unaccented note following the accented note on which the actual
cadence mostly occurs. Such feminine endings are very common,
both in phrases and sentences.

29. It is by no means necessary that the first phrase of a
sentence should end with a half cadence, as in the examples
hitherto given. Any form of middle cadence (*Counterpoint*, § 480)
may be employed. We give a few examples of the more common
middle cadences.

Here the cadence at the fourth bar is a full cadence (V^7a, Ia) ;
but the effect of finality is avoided by taking the third of the tonic
chord in the upper part.

30. In the following passage—

the first phrase ends on the third of the subdominant chord, the

harmonizing of the last two notes being I*a*, IV*a*. It will be
noticed that the sentence contains only four bars, instead of eight
as hitherto, and the phrases only two bars each instead of four.
This is because the passage is written in quadruple time, instead
of in duple. Each bar now contains two accents instead of one,
and the total number of accents in the sentence is the same as in
the examples previously quoted. We shall return to this point,
which is of considerable importance, later.

31. We next give an example of a sentence in which the first
phrase ends with an interrupted cadence.

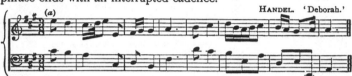

We have given Handel's bass as well as his melody here, because
the first phrase might have been harmonized with a full cadence
at the fourth bar; in this case there would *not* have been two
short sentences of four bars each, because a sentence must
contain at least two phrases (§ 24). Such a construction is
sometimes to be found, as in the following choral—

Here we have indicated the best harmonies for the cadences.
It is much better to treat the B in the third bar as part of the
chord of VII*b* than to take V*a* I*a* at the end of each phrase,
though either is possible.

32. We have just said that the first phrase of a sentence may
end with a full cadence. But, when this is the case, we generally
find that there is a modulation introduced in the course of the
sentence, and that the first phrase ends in a different key from the
second. The most usual modulation in a short sentence will
be into the key of the dominant, if the piece is in a major key,
and to the relative major, if in a minor key. We give an example
of each by Beethoven.

BEETHOVEN. Concerto in G, Op. 58.

33. As an example of a less frequent modulation for the first phrase, we give the following—

WEBER. 'Kampf und Sieg.

Here the modulation is to the relative minor of the subdominant. Notice also that the close of the sentence is here less decided than in the examples hitherto given, partly because it ends with the third of the tonic in the upper voice, but still more because the tonic chord is deferred by the feminine ending spoken of above (§ 28).

34. It is by no means uncommon for a sentence itself (sometimes as the opening sentence of a movement) to end with a modulation.

HAYDN. Symphony in D.

Here the first phrase ends with a half cadence in the tonic key, and the sentence ends with a full cadence in the dominant key.

In this sentence the first phrase ends, like the preceding, with a half cadence; the modulation is now to the relative minor of the dominant—a case of somewhat rare occurrence.

In this example, in a minor key, the first phrase ends with an inverted cadence in the tonic (Vb Ia), and the sentence closes with a full cadence in the relative major.

35. When the sentence ends with a modulation, the first phrase sometimes contains a full cadence (Va Ia) in the tonic key.

Here the second phrase begins with a transient modulation to the relative minor. In general, when the first phrase ends with a full

·cadence, the third of the tonic chord is, as here, placed in the upper part, to avoid the feeling of finality produced if the tonic itself is at the top. Sometimes, though more rarely, the tonic is found in the upper part, as in the following passage by Haydn—

36. We saw in § 30 a sentence only four bars in length, divided into two phrases of two bars each ; and we explained that this was because the time was *quadruple*, containing two accents in each bar, instead of only one. Every bar of $\frac{4}{4}$ time is in reality two bars of $\frac{2}{4}$ thrown into one, and is therefore a COMPOUND bar. In England the term 'compound time' is usually restricted to those bars which contain two or more bars of *triple* time, and we frequently find it defined as "that in which each beat is of the value of a dotted note." But the German definition, "a larger bar composed of two or more smaller bars" is far more accurate ; and it is, indeed, necessary for the proper understanding of rhythm that we should regard quadruple time in many cases as compound time. The reason is that the two accents in a bar of quadruple time are not of the same strength. Every beginner is taught that in $\frac{4}{4}$ time there is a strong accent on the first beat of the bar, and a weaker accent on the third ; and it is needful to bear this in mind in all compound times in order to get the cadences in the right positions.

37. Every student knows, or ought to know, that in a cadence in common time the last chord should come upon a strong accent. The chief exception to this rule is in the case of the "feminine endings" of which we gave an example in § 33, and of which other specimens may be seen in *Counterpoint*, § 483. The numerous instances to be found in the works of the great ·composers, of the final chord of a cadence occurring in quadruple time on the third beat of the bar instead of the first, are in the majority of cases due to the fact of the bar-lines being put in the wrong places throughout the whole piece. This arises simply

from inattention on the part of composers, who are often
indifferent, so long as the cadence comes on an accent, whether
that accent is strong or weak.   An example of this, as striking as
it is familiar, may be seen in Schubert's popular Impromptu in
B flat, Op. 142, No. 3.

SCHUBERT. Impromptu, Op. 142, No. 3.

Here the cadences in each case come on the third beat of the bar,
whereas the piece ought to begin with a half bar.   This is most
conclusively proved by the final cadence in the 15th and 16th
bars—

This cannot possibly be correct, as here written, for it violates one
of the strictest rules as to the treatment of a $\frac{6}{4}$ chord,—that when
it is followed by another chord on the same bass note, it must not
be on a weaker accent than the chord that follows it (*Harmony*,
§ 189).   But by changing the position of the bar-lines, the
passage becomes correct and intelligible at once.

Such instances of misplaced bar-lines are by no means uncommon
in compound time.   Dr. Riemann in his 'Catechismus der
Phrasierung' proves that the whole of Chopin's well-known
Nocturne in E flat (Op. 9, No. 2) is wrongly barred.

38. We said just now (§ 36) that every bar of quadruple time consisted of two bars of duple time thrown into one. We know that a bar of quadruple time contains a strong accent on the first beat and a weaker accent on the third. It is therefore composed of an accented and an (in comparison) unaccented bar. This brings us to our next point, and one of great importance. *Every musical sentence, or part of a sentence, is made by an alternation of accented and unaccented bars.* In the majority of cases, these follow one another with regularity—one accented, and one unaccented—this being the most natural arrangement, as we have already seen with accents (§ 26). Cases of departure from this general rule will be treated of in a later chapter of this volume; for the present we are concerned only with sentences in which the alternations of accent and non-accent are quite regular.

39. It is of the utmost importance, in fact indispensable, in investigating rhythms, to be able to determine with certainty which bars of a phrase, or sentence, are accented, and which unaccented. For this we have a very easy rule to guide us :—the bar in which a cadence occurs, ending the phrase or sentence, is always (except sometimes with feminine endings) an accented bar, and in the large majority of pieces it is only necessary to *count back* from this point, and to reckon every alternate bar as an accented one till we reach the beginning of the phrase.

40. An example will make this quite clear. We choose a scherzo by Beethoven, because here the time is so rapid that there can be no question of any secondary accent in the bar, such as is sometimes found in slow movements of $\frac{3}{4}$ time.

This passage, and indeed the whole scherzo, is very often played incorrectly, beginning with an accented bar. It is almost impossible to play it without accenting some of the bars more strongly than others, as the student will easily find if he tries to do so. To show which are the correct bars to accent, we will put two bars into one, and write the passage in $\frac{6}{4}$ time, which will give us a stronger and a weaker accent in each bar. If we accent the first, third, fifth, and seventh bars, we get this result—

Here the cadence is evidently wrong; for the dominant chord is
on the strong, and the tonic on the weak accent. It is quite clear
that the correct reading is to accent the second, fourth, sixth, and
eighth bars; we then have the following—

The form is now perfectly satisfactory. If the student will play
the whole scherzo, placing the accents as we have indicated, he
will find the same regularity in the position of the cadences
throughout. The silent bar just before the trio is then seen to be
a necessity to preserve the rhythm. We quote the last six bars of
the scherzo, and the beginning of the trio, writing it, as before in
$\frac{6}{4}$ time.

It will be seen that if we adopt any other accentuation than that
here indicated, the cadences will come in the wrong places
throughout the whole movement. Let it be said in passing
that the $\frac{6}{4}$ time we have here given is not, as it is commonly
described "compound common time," but *compound triple* time,
for it is made by putting two bars of triple time into one. A true
compound common time would be $\frac{4}{2}$, $\frac{4}{4}$, or $\frac{4}{8}$, made by putting
two bars of *duple* time into one.

41. Many similar illustrations might be given of the importance of distinguishing between accented and unaccented bars.

We refer the student, as especially striking examples, to the scherzos
in Beethoven's sonatas in C, Op. 2, No. 3, and E flat, Op. 27,
No. 1, in both of which the effect is entirely ruined by accenting
the wrong bars.   In each case he will be able to find the right
accentuation by reckoning backward from the cadences, as
explained above.   It should be added that it is not every passage
that can be so simply analyzed ; we often meet with more complex
rhythms, as we shall see later ; but in probably the majority
of cases, especially with older music, the simple rule here given
will be found sufficient.

42. .We have now to speak of sentences which contain more
than two phrases, or more than eight simple bars, or four
compound bars (§ 36), but in which the subdivision into phrases
of four bars is to be distinctly seen.   Sentences containing three
phrases are less common than those which contain four, most
probably because as the third phrase has no following phrase to
balance it, the natural feeling of proportion is somewhat disturbed.
Numerous examples may nevertheless be found, a very familiar one
being the first part of "God save the Queen," which consists
of three phrases of two bars each.   A very good example of this
construction will be seen in the following commencement of an
old German melody, the composer of which is unknown.

Old German Melody.

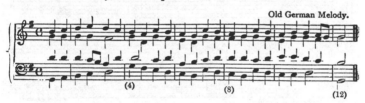

Here, though there only six bar-lines, there are in reality twelve
bars, as each bar is 'compound,' containing two accents.   We
have therefore reckoned this as a twelve-bar passage, and have
numbered the fourth, eighth, and twelfth bars, as being those
which contain the cadences.   The first phrase, of four bars, ends
with an inverted half cadence, the second, at bar 8, has an
inverted cadence, and the third a full cadence in the tonic key.

43. Our next example is taken from one of Haydn's quartetts,
and illustrates some other points.

HAYDN.   Quartett, Op. 17, No. 6.

Here we see at bar 4 a full cadence on a tonic pedal. Observe that the feeling of finality is avoided here in two ways—first by placing the third of the tonic at the top of the chord (§ 35), and secondly by the feminine ending (§ 28), which defers the appearance of the tonic chord till the unaccented beat of the bar. At bar 8 we have an ordinary half cadence, with both chords in their root position; and the sentence ends with a full cadence in the key of the dominant above a tonic pedal in that key.

44. Sentences consisting of four phrases are far more common than those with three. In these we find a more perfect symmetry, the first phrase being answered by the second, and the third by the fourth, or else (and perhaps quite as frequently) the first by the third, and the second by the fourth. Our examples will show both these varieties.

HAYDN. Quartett, Op. 55, No. 3.

Here the four-bar phrases are very clearly defined by the rests that follow them. The first and third are in unison. In such cases, we must always think of the implied harmony. The E♮ in the fourth bar must be here either the leading note in the key of F, or the third of the supertonic chromatic chord in B flat. Its being followed immediately by E♭ in bar 5, proves it to be the latter; and the implied harmony of bars 3 and 4 is probably something like this—

Though neither of these are recognized cadences in B flat, either would be an inverted half cadence in F; and though the key of F is not confirmed by what follows, there is sufficient cadential character in the passage to mark the division of the phrases. Similar reasoning will apply to the answering phrase (bars 9 to 12). Here the A♮ must be regarded as the sub-mediant of C minor, in which key the fourth phrase (at bar 13) unmistakably begins. The half cadence at bar 8 is replied to by the full cadence at bar 16, completing the sentence, which is perfectly symmetrical in form.

45. Our next illustration is rather more complex in construction.

MOZART. Symphony in D.

Here it is quite evident that the sentence ends with the full cadence at the sixteenth bar, while it is no less clear that it is divided into two equal parts by the half cadence (with a feminine ending) at bar 8. So far, therefore, it is quite regular But if we try further subdivision, we see that there is no cadence at bars 4 and 12, for a chord of the dominant seventh does not suggest a cadence. Evidently the subdivision here comes on the resolution of the discords—that is, in bars 5 and 13; so that the two halves of the sentence appear to divide into two unequal portions of five bars and three. But, as we shall learn in the next chapter, the first note of the melody here does not form part of the first phrase, which really begins on the sixth quaver, E, and extends to the first note of bar 5. The phrase is

It will be seen that it contains four strong accents. The second phrase *begins at the end of the first one ;* and bar 5 is at the same time the last bar of the first phrase, and the first bar of the second. The second phrase is

Like the first it contains four strong accents. Here we see for the first time an example of the overlapping of two phrases—a thing of very frequent occurrence, of which we shall find numerous examples when we come to deal with less regular and more complex rhythms. The second half of this sentence, it will be seen, is the exact counterpart of the first half.

46. We will now give another variety of the sixteen-bar sentence.

WAGNER. 'Tannhäuser.'

Here the sentence is completed at the sixteenth bar, and there is a half cadence, with a feminine ending, at the eighth bar. But if we examine these two halves, we find that while the first divides at the fourth bar with an irregular cadence—supertonic preceded by first inversion of tonic—the second half does not divide at all, for there is nothing in it which can be considered as a sufficient cadence. Here we have another very common case—an eight-bar phrase which divides into two fours is answered by another eight-bar phrase which is indivisible. The balance of the whole sentence is perfectly regular—

$$4 + 4 + 8 = 16.$$

This point will be treated of in a later chapter of this volume; all we are now concerned with is the showing different kinds of sixteen-bar sentences of regular construction.

47. Our last example will be a well-known passage in 'Lohengrin'—

Wagner. 'Lohengrin.'

(16)

If we examine the melody of the upper part alone, we shall see it begins with two phrases of four bars each, like the passage quoted in the last paragraph from the 'Tannhäuser' overture; these eight bars are answered by another eight bars, indivisible into two fours. So far the two passages resemble one another; but there is an important difference in the fact that here the phrases at bars 4 and 8 are less clearly marked off, because in the half cadences the seventh is added to the dominant harmony. The construction of the melody prevents our regarding the tonic chords in bars 5 and 9 as belonging to the preceding phrases, as we did in the extract from Mozart in § 45; we must therefore regard this as a sixteen-bar sentence, the different phrases of which are more closely connected than usual. Observe that here it is the *second* phrase which answers the first, instead of the *third* as in §§ 44, 45. In spite of there being no full cadence at the eighth bar, it is often advisable to consider an eight-bar period as a *sentence*, even though it may end with a half cadence. This is because the eight-bar formation, as we have already seen (§§ 25, 26), is the *normal* one; and it would greatly complicate our analyses, if we some-times counted up to eight bars, and at other times to sixteen. It will be needful to bear this in mind in the later chapters of this volume.

48. We have now given enough examples of various kinds to enable the student to understand the nature of a musical sentence in which the rhythm is regular. We next proceed to show how a sentence can be further subdivided.

CHAPTER III.

THE SUBDIVISIONS OF A MUSICAL SENTENCE—SECTIONS AND MOTIVES.

49. In the last chapter we explained the nature of a musical sentence, and we showed that it ended with some form of full cadence, and that it was divisible into at least two parts, called phrases. We have now to show that these phrases are themselves subdivisible, and we shall (to use a mathematical expression) reduce them to their lowest terms. For this purpose we will take a few of the simple sentences given in the last chapter, and analyze them more minutely.

50. Let us first take the two lines of the choral quoted in § 24. It will be remembered that the eight-bar sentence is divided by the half cadence into two four-bar phrases, which we will call, to distinguish them, the "fore-phrase" and the "after-phrase." *

Here the after-phrase is the response to the fore-phrase ; and just as the full cadence at bar 8 has a feeling of greater completeness than the half cadence at bar 4, the whole second phrase is felt to be more *weighty* than the first. We saw in the last chapter that a phrase contained accented and unaccented bars (§§ 38, 39). By an extension of the same principle we may now say that a sentence contains accented and unaccented phrases. This important relation of accent and non-accent applies alike to the smaller and larger divisions of the music.

51. Now let us take these phrases, and try to subdivide them further. As each phrase contains four complete bars, the natural division would seem at first sight to be into two halves of two bars each—

These halves of a phrase we call SECTIONS. But if we take these sections separately, we find that the first and third have a very

---

* These terms are used as the English equivalents of the German expressions "Vordersatz" and "Nachsatz.'

incomplete and unsatisfactory effect.   The reason of this is partly
because they end on an unaccented note.   We shall see later in
this chapter that it is possible *under certain conditions* for the
smaller sub-divisions of a sentence to end on an unaccented note ;
but we shall also see that those conditions are not present here.
But the chief reason why the division into sections here given is
so unsatisfactory is, that the notes D and A at the end of bars 2
and 6 are so evidently closely connected with, and leading up to
the following accented notes, C and G.   It is quite clear that the
proper division of these phrases into sections is the following—

Observe that although each phrase is now divided unequally—into
two sections of one-and-a-half and two-and-a-half bars respectively,
the balance of the music is in no degree disturbed, because each
section contains, as before, two accents.

52. An additional proof of the correctness of the sectional
divisions we have here given is furnished by the fact that we can
now put cadences (of course only *middle* cadences) at the end of
each section.   This will be seen if we harmonize the sentence in
the simplest way.

It is evident that there is no point of repose *at the end* of the
second and sixth bars, while the inverted cadence in the second
bar, and the interrupted cadence in the sixth, furnish us with
resting places, and unmistakably indicate the points at which the
phrases should be subdivided.

53. It is not every phrase which will divide into two sections.
In some of the examples of sentences given in the last chapter
(§§ 46, 47), we saw how two phrases of four bars each were
answered by one phrase of eight bars, thus obtaining variety
without destroying the balance of the whole.   In the same way we
very often find that if the fore-phrase is divided into sections the
after-phrase is indivisible, as in the following example :—

BEETHOVEN.   Sonata, Op. 2, No. 1.

54. Sometimes, though not so frequently, the after-phrase is divided into sections, while the fore-phrase is undivided. This is the case in the commencement of the air "I will sing of Thy great mercies," in 'St. Paul.'

MENDELSSOHN. 'St. Paul.'

The fact that the second phrase ends with a half cadence, and therefore does not complete the sentence, makes no difference for our purpose, as we are quoting the passage simply to show the alternation of phrases which are and are not divisible into sections. Looking at the fore-phrase, the student may ask, why can there not be the end of a section after the first note in the second bar? The answer is, that Mendelssohn has harmonized the passage in such a way that there is no possible break in the bar, as will be seen by referring to the oratorio; and in subdividing phrases, harmonic considerations are of much importance, as we found in the last chapter in determining the limits of the phrases themselves. We shall deal with this point later in the chapter.

55. It is not necessary—indeed it is often unadvisable—that the cadential feeling should be as marked at the end of a section as at the end of a phrase. If it were, the continuity of the music would frequently be destroyed, and we should have the effect of continual halting. In our example in § 52 the cadences at the end of the first and third sections have a much more incomplete character than those at the ends of the phrases. We often find, therefore, that an eight-bar phrase which cannot be subdivided into two four-bar phrases can yet be divided into four two-bar sections. This is the case in the example from the overture to 'Tannhäuser,' that we gave in the last chapter (§ 46). It will be remembered that it consists of two four-bar phrases followed by one of eight bars. The latter, which begins on the last crotchet of bar 8, divides into four sections thus—

WAGNER. Tannhäuser.'

The reasons for the points at which we make the divisions will be seen when we come presently to speak of *motives.*

56. We will now take another of our examples from the last chapter—that by Haydn, given in § 29—and divide it into

sections.   For the sake of clearness, we now give the harmony as
well as the melody.

HAYDN.   Symphony in G.

Here the subdivisions are much more distinctly marked by the
cadences than in the passages we have been examining.   The fore-
phrase, as we saw in the last chapter, ends with a full cadence, the
effect of finality being avoided by the feminine ending—deferring
the tonic chord to the unaccented half of the bar—and by putting
the third of the tonic chord in the upper part.   This phrase is
divided into two sections of exactly equal length, the first of
which ends with a full cadence.   Notice that, although the section
extends to the second beat of the bar, there is no feminine
ending here, nor at the end of the sentence, because the repetition
of the G is equivalent, both melodically and harmonically, to one
G held as a dotted crotchet.   The cadence is on the accented
beat at the beginning of the bar.   The after-phrase is no less
clearly divided into two sections by a half cadence; and the
student will see how beautifully symmetrical the whole sentence
is, in spite of the small variety of cadences used.

57. We recommend the student to examine the other sentences
given in the last chapter, and to try to divide them into sections
for himself.   He will be well repaid for his trouble.

58. There is still one more subdivision possible.   Every
section contains at least two accents, and can be separated into
smaller parts, containing only one accent each.   Such parts are
called MOTIVES,* and correspond exactly to the *feet* in poetry
(§ 21).   Here we have what (to borrow a scientific term) we may
call the "protoplasm"—the germ out of which all music springs.
A thorough knowledge of the nature of the motive is therefore
indispensable to anyone who would understand the fundamental
principles of musical form.

---

* The word "motive" is the Anglicized form of the German ' *Motif*,' and must
be pronounced, not like the ' motive' which induces an action, but with the accent
on the second syllable, as if it were spelt ' *Moteeve.*'

59. Let us once more return to the choral which we have already divided into phrases and sections (§ 51), and try to subdivide the sections into motives. We have seen in the case of the sections, that the second section, which terminates a phrase, has a feeling of greater completeness than the first. The centre of gravity, so to speak, lies in the second half. We have seen this also in the case of the phrases themselves—the after-phrase (or *responsive* phrase) has a feeling of completeness lacking to the fore-phrase, which calls for something to follow it. In other words, *response implies accent.* The ordinary full cadence illustrates the same point. If we put the dominant chord on the accented beat, and the following tonic chord on the unaccented, there is no feeling of finality. To obtain a satisfactory effect we have to connect an unaccented (or less accented) dominant chord with an accented tonic chord.

Here, then, is the general principle which must guide us :—With certain exceptions, to be presently noted, every unaccented note is to be regarded in its connexion with the following, and not with the preceding accented note. An accented note preceded by an unaccented note, as in the cadence above, gives us the simplest possible form of the motive.

60. We will now take the choral, which we have already divided into sections in § 51 (*b*), and divide it into motives. We have just said that an accented note preceded by an unaccented note gives the simplest form of motive. But the choral we are now analyzing begins with an accented note not preceded by any unaccented note. Is the first note therefore a motive by itself? Certainly not; a motive must contain at least two notes,* or we do not get the relation of accent and non-accent. But it is extremely common to find a phrase or sentence beginning with an accented note, which must be considered as an incomplete motive, serving as a point of departure. We may term this the *elision* of the unaccented part of the motive.

61. We now divide the sentence into motives; it will be seen that the second phrase, like the first, begins with an incomplete motive—a new point of departure.

The sign ⌐ indicates an incomplete motive. To prove that this is the correct division, it is only necessary to shorten the accented notes, and to follow them by rests :—

* It is however quite possible for these two notes to be the same note, either repeated, or even tied, as in the example to § 71, later in this chapter.

If, on the other hand the unaccented note ought to be connected, not with the following, but with the preceding accented note to form a motive, and we adopt the same process of shortening the second note, we obtain the following—

Everyone's musical feeling will tell him at once that this division is incorrect, and that the breaks come in the wrong places.

62. Before proceeding to lay down any general principles, we will analyze another sentence, in which the motives are much less simple. We will take the passage by Beethoven quoted in § 53.

BEETHOVEN. Sonata, Op. 2, No. 1.

We have quoted only the melody, because every student may be reasonably presumed to have a copy of Beethoven's sonatas, and can see the harmony (to which we shall have to refer) for himself. It will be remembered that the sentence consists of two phrases, of which the fore-phrase is divided into two sections, while the after-phrase is undivided.

63. As the sentence begins on an unaccented beat, the first motive is a complete one, ending with the crotchet A. The second motive completes the first section, and extends to the first E in the second bar. That the section does not end on the crotchet F is clearly proved by the harmony, which shows a half cadence ($^6_4$ $^5_3$) with a feminine ending. In the case of a feminine ending (whether such as we find here, or with a suspension or an appoggiatura), a motive will always end on an unaccented note. In any other case, it will end with an accented note, unless it can be seen from the comparison with other similar motives that the following motive does not begin immediately after the accented note. An example will illustrate this point.

WEBER. 'Oberon.'

Here the sentence begins with an incomplete motive, without the first up-beat (the "point of departure" § 60). That the following

notes, A and F, do not form part of the second motive, is proved
by an examination of the passage, which is founded, excepting
the commencement of each phrase, on a motive of three notes,
seen most clearly in the last three bars of the sentence. The
modifications, both in melody and length of notes, which the
motive undergoes will be explained in a later chapter. The
sentence therefore begins with an incomplete motive with a
feminine ending.

64. It should be most clearly understood that we are never
justified in assuming a feminine ending to a motive, unless the
harmony (as in the second bar of the example in § 62) or the
context (as in the passage from Weber just given) unmistakably
shows that the unaccented note belongs to the preceding accented
one. Returning now to our example from Beethoven, what we
have just said explains our marking the third motive as ending on
F, though the following C belongs to the same harmony. It is
only by consistently following out this system that we are able to
explain some of the progressions to be found in the works of the
great masters. Dr. Riemann has admirably shown this in the
case of the apparent consecutive fifths in a well-known passage in
Bach's Organ Toccata in D minor—

BACH. Toccata in D minor.

Here it looks at first sight as if the harmonic progression were the
following, the effect of which is horrible :

But when we subdivide it into motives, we see at once that the
implied harmony is quite correct.

Observe that the feminine ending here is proved by the motive

in which it is needful to include the A, as the resolution of the
seventh, B; this illustrates what has been said as to the importance
of harmonic considerations in deciding the limits of a motive.

As the whole passage is sequential, the other motives necessarily
have the same form.

65. We now give another example, illustrating a somewhat
different point, but showing no less clearly the necessity of
regarding unaccented notes in their relation to the following
accented.

SCHUMANN.   Trio in F, Op. 80.

Here it looks on a cursory inspection as if the second of each
group of quavers were a passing note wrongly quitted by leap.
But as soon as we divide the quaver passage into motives,

we see that the second quaver belongs to the following harmony,
and is in fact an anticipation, at an octave's distance, of the
immediately succeeding crotchet in the upper part. Such passages
as these furnish conclusive proof of the correctness of the rules
here laid down as to the nature of the motive.

66. It will not be necessary, after what has been already said
to analyze the remaining motives of the passage in § 62 one by
one.   The student will be easily able to understand them for
himself.   But there is one very important caution to be given.
He is not to suppose that any break is of necessity to be made,
even in thought, much less in performance, between one motive
and the next.   The points of rest are at the ends of sentences
and phrases, and sometimes (though not invariably, and always to
a less extent) at the ends of sections.   Speaking roughly, these
divisions may be compared to the stops in punctuation.   The end
of a sentence corresponds to a full stop, that of a phrase to a
semicolon, and of a section to a comma.   This must not be taken

as more than an attempt, and necessarily a rough one, to show the analogy between musical and literary composition. But the motives are the equivalents of musical *feet;* and it would be just as absurd to make, or to think of, a break after every motive as it would be to pause after every foot in reading poetry. We are at present only *analyzing* musical sentences; it is when we come later to construct them for ourselves that we shall feel the true importance, and the real functions of the motive.

67. Before proceeding further, we will take one more example —the sentence by Haydn given in § 56, and divide it into motives. It is only necessary to give the melody.

HAYDN.   Symphony in G.

Instead of analyzing this for the student, it will be better to leave him to examine it for himself, and to see why the divisions of the motives are where he finds them.

68. There is one more point still to be noticed. Some of these motives are capable of further subdivision. For example, the fourth can be divided thus—

Such subdivisions are not uncommon, especially in motives which are in slow *tempo,* and contain many notes. These parts of a motive we will call *Sub-motives;* if we consider the motives as musical words, the sub-motives are the syllables.

69. We are now in a position to give an intelligible definition of a motive. We give it in the following words :

A MOTIVE is composed of a strongly accented note, preceded by one or more unaccented or less accented notes, and followed by unaccented notes, only when the harmony requires it, or the context shows that the following motive does not begin immediately after the accent.

70. In quick music, with sometimes only one note in the bar, the motive will consist of two bars. Thus the motives in the scherzo of Beethoven quoted in § 40 will be the following :

BEETHOVEN.   Sonata, Op. 28.

It will be seen that the third motive has a feminine ending, but that the fourth has not, as there is merely a repetition of the same

notes.   Let it be noticed that the framework of the third and
fourth motives is the same which we have already given (§ 59)
as the simplest possible form of the motive.

71. A striking proof of the correctness of the rule laid down
at the beginning of the last section is furnished by the trio in the
scherzo of Beethoven's quartett in E flat, Op. 74, of which we give
the first bars.

It is quite evident that the motives in the viola part must be
as here marked, for the cadence must come on an accented bar
(§ 39), and therefore indicate the end of a motive.   No single
note will form a motive; we therefore count back, taking each
accented bar as the end of a motive, till we come to the beginning
of the passage.   But with the violoncello part the limits of the
motives are not at first sight so clear; for we often have motives
of different lengths going on simultaneously.   We might therefore
be in doubt whether the motives in the bass should not be
marked thus—

But Beethoven has clearly indicated his intentions here.   At the
beginning of the trio he writes "Si ha s' immaginar la battuta

di $\frac{6}{8}$," that is, "we have to imagine $\frac{6}{8}$ time"—in other words, to throw two bars into one, and think of the crotchets as if they were quavers. Now in rapid $\frac{6}{8}$ time, "almost *prestissimo*," as here marked, there will only be one accent in the bar, consequently only one motive, extending over two bars *as here written*, but which, we know from Beethoven himself, are here equivalent to one.

72. We give one more example of a different kind, showing the two-bar motive with feminine endings. It is the commencement of No. 6 of Schubert's 'Momens Musicals.' The first sentence contains sixteen bars, with only one beat in each, and therefore equivalent to the eight-bar sentence with two beats in a bar of which we have seen so many examples in the last chapter. We number the accented bars throughout. As the piece is universally accessible, it will be sufficient to give the melody.

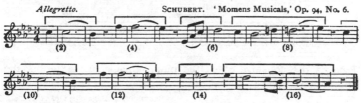

Here we see an ordinary eight-bar sentence, each bar being divided into two. The figures 2, 4, 6, 8, &c., therefore really show the position of the strong accent of each bar, and the special point to be noticed is that six out of eight motives have feminine endings. To make this clear, we write the passage (as we did that by Beethoven in § 40) in $\frac{6}{4}$ time.

The construction will now be seen to be quite regular.

73. Let us now examine the constituents of a motive. These are three in number. The notes composing a motive may vary in pitch, in duration of time, and in accent. Of these constituents the last is by far the most important, and is indeed indispensable. A motive must consist of at least two notes, of which one will be accented, and the other unaccented. Even if each note fills a whole bar, and therefore begins on an accented beat, the larger time-measurement ("metre") comes into operation, and we have

an accented and an unaccented bar, as in our examples in §§ 40 and 71. In the majority of cases, variety of pitch and of time-duration are also to be found, as will be seen by examining the various motives in our examples. But either or both of these can be dispensed with, as will appear from the following extracts from familiar works.

WEBER.   Sonata in C, Op. 24.

In this passage there is plenty of variety of pitch, but the motives are composed of notes of exactly the same time-value.

BEETHOVEN.   Quartett in F, Op. 59, No. 1.

Here is the converse case; the pitch remains the same, but the length of the notes varies.

BEETHOVEN.   Bagatelle, Op. 33, No. 7.

As the fifth, sixth, and seventh bars of this passage contain in the upper parts only one note each, we have here evidently two-bar motives. If we examine the second motive (bars 2 to 4), we see that neither pitch nor length of notes varies, but the indispensable attribute, *accent* remains. There is a weaker accent at the beginning of the third bar, dividing the motive into two sub-motives, and a strong accent on the last note of the motive.

74. Before proceeding to the next division of our subject, it will be advisable to summarize as clearly and concisely as we can the important general principles that have been laid down in this and the preceding chapter.

I. By *Rhythm* is meant the system on which the cadences in a composition are placed. If these cadences come at equal distances through a piece, or portion of a piece, such piece, or portion of a piece, is said to be "in regular rhythm"; if the cadences come at unequal distances, the rhythm is irregular. By far the most common arrangement of cadences is at distances of two, four, or eight bars. A piece in which the cadences fall at these distances is said to be "in two-, four-, or eight-bar rhythm," as the case may be.

II. A portion of a composition usually ending with a full cadence, and divided by one or more middle cadences into at least two parts, is called a *Sentence*, or *Period*. It is not necessary that in the final tonic chord of the cadence at the end of a sentence the root should be in the upper voice, though in the majority of instances this will probably be found to be the case; it is also possible for the sentence to terminate with a feminine ending, the tonic chord being on the less accented beat (see example § 33), or even to end with a half cadence (§ 47).

III. The first subdivision of a musical sentence is into *Phrases*. There is no restriction as to the number of phrases composing a sentence. There must be at least two, because without the balance, or counterpoise, given by the responsive phrase, there is no feeling of completeness in the sentence. The majority of sentences will contain either two or four phrases. A phrase will almost always end with a cadence of some kind; this may be either a full, half, inverted, or interrupted cadence, occasionally a phrase ends on a discord (§ 47). A full cadence in the tonic key will be rarely found as a middle cadence, unless the sentence ends with a modulation.

IV. In many cases, though not invariably, the phrases will themselves be divisible into *Sections*. Though it is possible for even a section to end with a full cadence (see example, § 56), we mostly find the cadential effect less distinct in a section than in a phrase. Very often, if a sentence consists of two phrases, one of these will be subdivisible into two sections, while the other is indivisible. By this means variety of detail is obtained without the sacrifice of symmetry.

V. If we further subdivide phrases or sections into small portions containing one strong accent each, we have *Motives*. Except in the cases mentioned in § 63, unaccented notes always form part of the same motive as the next accented note which follows them. When a sentence, or phrase, begins (as is often the case) with an accented note, such note is an incomplete motive, with elision of its unaccented notes. It is possible for such a motive to have a feminine ending (see the example in § 63), in which · case it looks like, but is not in reality, a motive with reversed accents.

VI. Just as a bar consists of an alternation of accented and unaccented beats, a sentence or phrase contains an alternation of accented and unaccented bars. To determine which are the accented bars, examine the cadences, and remember that the last note of a cadence, except where there is a feminine ending, always comes on an accented bar.   In rapid *tempo*, with only one beat in a bar (see examples §§ 71, 73), a motive will often extend over two bars.

75. It must be understood that the principles here laid down apply fully only to sentences which are perfectly regular in their construction.   It is only of such that we have been speaking in these chapters.   More complex and irregular rhythms are often to be met with : these will be' treated of in a later chapter of this volume.

CHAPTER IV

MODULATION—KEY-RELATIONSHIP.

76. In the preceding chapters we have explained the nature of a musical sentence, or period, and have shown how it can be divided into phrases, sections, and motives. We have seen that in many sentences, even in those that are quite short, modulations are employed, and are indeed often most useful. Before proceeding to show the student how to construct musical sentences for himself, it will therefore be advisable to deal with the whole question of modulation—a very large subject, as will be seen, but a thorough knowledge of which is indispensable to anyone who wishes to compose. The matter has been partially treated of in *Harmony*, Chapter IX., and referred to incidentally in later parts of the same volume. It will now be needful to enter upon its discussion more systematically; and we shall be obliged to repeat, for the sake of clearness, some few things with which the student will be already familiar.

77. By Modulation is simply meant a change of key—that is. the temporary disestablishment of the original tonic, and the substitution of a new one in its place. If the substitution of the new tonic is only momentary, the modulation is said to be "a transient modulation," or, more briefly, "a transition." *

Here we see at (*a*) a modulation into D minor, returning in the next bar to the original key. At (*b*) is a modulation to A minor, and at (*c*) to F major; but in no case are there more than two chords in the new key. As no single chord can ever define a key (*Harmony*, § 278), the modulations here are the briefest possible; they are therefore *transient* modulations, or *transitions*.

78. Here the student may naturally ask, How can we tell that at (*c*) there are only two chords in the key of F? for the B flat is

---

* Some writers use the word "transition" to signify a modulation to a remote key; but the sense in which we are here using it is more appropriate, and we shall therefore restrict it to cases in which any new key (whether related or not) is only momentarily touched on.

D

not contradicted by a B natural till later. Why may not the third and fourth chords from the end be also considered to belong to the key of F, as they contain no notes foreign to the signature of that key?

79. The answer to this question illustrates the importance of considering the division of a sentence into the motives spoken of in the last chapter. It is quite clear that the third and fourth chords from the end form part of the same motive, and will therefore be in the same key. It is true that they *might* both be in the key of F. But if the $\frac{6}{4}$ on G were in the key of F, it would be the second inversion of the dominant chord, which cannot be used cadentially—that is, followed by another chord on the same bass note or its octave (*Harmony*, § 177). It is evident from what follows that this chord is here in the key of C; consequently we regard the unaccented chord of the same motive as being also in that key, and there are only two chords in the key of F.

80. The first question with which we have to deal is that of key-relationship. On this point we quote the definition given in *Harmony* (§ 272)—"Two major keys are said to be related to one another when their tonics are consonant; and the more perfect the consonance the nearer the relationship." To this we now add, that the more nearly the keys are related, the more chords they will have in common. This will be clearly seen later, when we come to speak of the chords common to any two keys; for the present we leave out of consideration all discords and chromatic chords. It is evident that the nearest related major keys to C are F and G, because their tonics form perfect consonances with C; and, as each key has only one note of its diatonic scale different from that of the scale of C, it is clear that each of these keys will have four diatonic triads common to itself and the key of C. For the same reason, A minor, having six of the seven notes of its diatonic scale common to itself and C, and therefore four diatonic triads in common, is a nearly related key to C; while the relative minors of F and G, though less closely connected with the key of C, are also included among the nearly related keys by reason of their close relationship to its dominant and subdominant.

81. We have just seen that, though the five keys G, F, A minor, E minor and D minor are all nearly related to C major, they are not all *equally* nearly related. The exact degree of relationship depends on the number of chords which they have in common. We find that, of diatonic triads (of which alone we are speaking at present), G, F, and A minor have four each in common with C, while E minor has only three, and D minor only one. By the addition of discords and chromatic harmonies, the number of chords in common will be considerably increased in each case; but D minor will still be the least nearly related of the

"attendant keys" of C, as this circle of related keys is often called, and E minor will come next in ascending order. This is probably the reason why a modulation from any major key to its supertonic minor is less often met with, especially as a first modulation, than one to any other of the nearly related keys. It must be understood that we are not referring to such merely transient modulations as those shown in our example, § 77, but to those more pronounced modulations where a phrase or sentence ends in the new key.

82. Let us now examine the nearly related keys to a minor key, and we shall obtain some different results. We make our circle of attendant keys on the same plan as with the major key— that is, we take the *minor* keys a perfect fifth above and below our tonic, and the relative majors of these three keys. But if, in order to determine the respective nearness of relationship of the different keys, we apply the same test as with the major keys, we shall find some striking differences in the results now obtained. Let us take A minor as our central tonic, because the whole circle of nearly related keys will be the same six as with C major. But whereas the keys a perfect fifth above and below C major had four chords each in common with it, the keys of E minor and D minor have but one chord each in common with A minor. The only key which has four chords in common with A minor is its relative major, C; this is therefore its most nearly related key. Next comes its submediant major, F—the relative major of its subdominant—with three chords in common; while G major (the relative major of the dominant, E minor) has, like D minor and E minor, only one chord common to itself and A minor. Again our theory as to nearness of relationship depending upon the number of chords common to the two keys agrees with the practice of composers; for we find that the most frequent modulations, especially as first modulations, from any minor key are to its relative major, or to its submediant major.

83. We must now examine those keys which stand in the second degree of relationship. Taking first the major keys, they will be those in which the tonics are still consonant, but in which the consonance is imperfect, instead of perfect. Taking, as before, C as our centre, the keys will be those at the distance of a major or minor third above or below it, viz: E, E flat, A, and A flat. Here the test of relationship we have hitherto applied fails us altogether, for there is not a single common chord which, *as a diatonic chord*, belongs to C and any one of the other keys we have just named. Evidently we must now look for some other bond of connexion.

84. Fortunately we have not to go far in order to find what we require. In major keys, the tonics of which are at a distance of a major or minor third from one another, we shall always find some triads which are diatonic in one of the two keys and

chromatic in the other. For example, the triads on the tonic, subdominant, and submediant of C major are all of them chromatic triads in E major (*Harmony*, Chapter XV.). Obviously the relation between the keys of A flat and C will be the same as between C and E, the tonics in both cases being a major third apart, and the chromatic triads on the minor second, the subdominant, and the minor sixth of C will all be diatonic in A flat.

85. If we now take keys whose tonics are a minor third apart—*e.g.*, C and A major, or C and E flat, we shall find similar connexions. The chords of the supertonic and subdominant of C are the chromatic chords on the subdominant and submediant of A, and the diminished triad on the leading note of C is the upper part of the dominant minor ninth of A. On the other hand, the diatonic chord on the subdominant of A is the chromatic chord on the supertonic of C. It will be evident that, as the relation between C and E flat is the same as that between A and C, we can work out a similar connexion of chords between these two keys also.

86. The number of triads common to two keys in the second degree of relationship can be increased if we include those in which an enharmonic change would be implied. For example, the dominant chord of A major, if we substitute A flat for G sharp, becomes the last inversion of one of the forms of the dominant thirteenth in C; and the dominant chord of E major, by a similar substitution of E flat for D sharp, becomes a supertonic major thirteenth in C. Examples of both these chords of the thirteenth, in the shape and with the notation here referred to, will be seen in *Harmony*, §§ 563, 564. But this possibility of bringing a chord into a new key by enharmonically changing one or more of its notes, though extremely useful, as will be seen later, for the purposes of modulation, does not affect the question of nearness or remoteness of key-relationship, for the very simple reason that it can be applied alike with related and with unrelated keys. We have mentioned it here, to show that there are more chords common to two keys in the second degree of relationship than would appear at a first glance.

87. We remember that with nearly related keys, the major keys of the dominant and subdominant bring their relative minors along with them into the circle of near relationship. But this is only partially the case with the relative minors of keys distant a third from what we may term the central tonic. In the group which we have been discussing, in which C is the centre, and the related major keys of the second degree are E, E flat, A, and A flat, it will be evident at once that the relative minors of these keys will not all stand upon the same footing. The key of C minor has so many chords common with C major that it is doubtful whether it ought not to be included among the most nearly related keys; while the key of F minor has several of its

most important chords (tonic, chromatic supertonic, and dominant) appearing either as diatonic or chromatic chords in the
key of C. On the other hand, the connexion between the key of
C and those of F sharp minor and C sharp minor is very remote,
for the few triads common to the keys are among those which,
either in the one key or the other, are the least frequently used,
as the student will easily discover on investigating the chords
common to the two keys. We arrive therefore at this result—
that only those relative minors of keys in the second degree of
relationship are themselves related to the central tonic which
contain more flats in the signature than the tonic.

88. We have already seen (§ 82) that among the nearly related
keys to a minor key the minors of its dominant and subdominant
were much less nearly related to the tonic than was the case with
the dominant and subdominant of a major key. In fact, all minor
keys are more loosely related to each other than major keys, and
the rule given above, that two major keys are related to one
another when their tonics are consonant, does not apply at all to
two minor keys in the second degree of relationship, that is, when
the tonics are at a distance of a third from one another.

89. Let us test this statement with the minor keys at a
distance of a major and minor third above and below A minor.
These will be C minor and C sharp minor above, and F minor
and F sharp minor below. Excluding (as we have done in other
cases) those chords which require an enharmonic change to take
them into one of the other keys, we find that the only triads in
A minor which are common to it and to either of the four keys we
have just named are the two diminished triads on the second and
seventh degrees of the scale. Of these the triad on the second
degree of the scale can also belong to the keys of C minor and
F minor, as part of the fundamental harmony of G, while the
diminished triad on G sharp can also belong to the keys of
C sharp and F sharp minor, as part of the fundamental harmony
of C sharp. Both triads in A minor are part of the dominant
harmony; in no case have we a *complete* chord; and this slight
point of contact is not enough to establish a relationship between
the keys

90. While, however, these minor keys are not themselves
related to the minor key whose tonic is at a distance of a third
from them, we shall nevertheless find that two of their relative
majors are related A little thought will show the student that
the relative majors of the *flatter* keys than A minor (E flat and
A flat) will be quite unrelated; but the relative majors of the
sharper keys, viz., A major and E major, will be just as closely
related as we saw in § 87 that the keys of C minor and F minor
were related to C major. The relationship is in fact identical.

91. It is an interesting point, and worth noticing as we pass,
that, in the relations we have just noticed, the minor key is the

exact converse of the major. In this second group of related
keys, the minors which are related to any tonic major are the
tonic minor and the subdominant minor—in other words, those
minor keys whose signature contains three and four *flats* more
than the original key ; while in the same group the related major
keys to any tonic minor are the tonic major and the dominant
major—the major keys whose signature contains three and four
sharps more than the original key. It will be seen that in all
cases of relationship in the second degree between a major and a
minor key, the tonics of the two keys will be consonant.

92. It should further be observed that we do not include the
dominant minor of a major key, nor the subdominant major of a
minor key, among the related keys, because the immediate juxtaposition of these keys produces a disturbing effect on the tonality.
This will be clearly seen if we put the two keys next to one
another, with one intermediate chord to make the modulation—

Here the modulation is effected at (*a*), as we shall explain in the
next chapter, by taking the chord of D major as the chromatic
chord on the supertonic of C, and quitting it as the dominant
chord of G minor. But the effect is unsatisfactory ; for it
suggests at the second and third bars either a major subdominant
chord in G minor, or a minor dominant chord in C. If we make
the converse modulation, from G minor to C, we shall have the
same unpleasant effect.

93. All other keys, whether major or minor, excepting those
already spoken of, are said to be "unrelated" keys. In the case
of two major keys, the want of relationship arises from the fact of
the tonics being dissonant (§ 80) ;· while the connexion of minor
keys is, as we have already seen, so much looser than that of
major ones, that in all other keys than those above considered the
points of contact are too slight to allow us to regard the keys as
related.

94. We conclude this chapter with a table of all related major
and minor keys—not now taking any one key as a centre, but
expressing the relationship of the tonics to one another according
to their intervals.

TABLE OF RELATED KEYS.

MAJOR KEYS.   MINOR KEYS.

(*a*) Nearly related.

Major Keys	Minor Keys
Dominant, *major*.	Mediant, *major*.
Subdominant, *major*.	Submediant, *major*.
Submediant, *minor*.	Dominant, *minor*.
Mediant, *minor*.	Subdominant, *minor*.
Supertonic, *minor*.	*Major* key of minor 7th.

(*b*) In the second degree of relationship.

Major Keys	Minor Keys
Mediant, *major*.	Tonic, *major*.
Flat mediant, *major*.	Dominant, *major*
Submediant, *major*.	
Flat submediant, *major*.	
Tonic, *minor*.	
Subdominant, *minor*.	

CHAPTER V

THE MEANS OF MODULATION—MODULATION BY MEANS OF TRIADS.

95. We have now to deal with the very important question, In what way is a modulation best effected between any two keys that may be named? This is a question which it is impossible to answer in a few words, or even in a few pages; nor, indeed, can anything more than a very general answer be given at all. For the means of modulation are in many cases practically almost exhaustless, especially between nearly related keys. In endeavouring to explain the methods of procedure we shall follow our usual plan of taking actual passages from the works of the great masters, analyzing them to see what course has been pursued, and trying to deduce a few general principles for the guidance of students.

96. In a very large majority of cases a modulation is effected by means of a chord common to the key quitted and to that entered. Even the simplest modulations to nearly related keys are mostly made in this way. As an example we give a short subject by Mozart.

MOZART.   Piano-Trio in G.

This theme consists of two sentences of eight bars each, each sentence being subdivided into two four-bar phrases. At (a) occurs a modulation into the key of the dominant. This is effected (*Harmony*, § 278) "by introducing a chord containing a note belonging to the new key, but foreign (*i.e.* as a *diatonic* note) to that which we are leaving, and by following that chord by other

chords defining and fixing the new key." Here F♯ is foreign to
the key-signature of C, but the student will be aware that the
chord at (a) might also be the chromatic supertonic chord in the
key of C. That it is not so here is proved by what follows.
The modulation is therefore effected by *taking* the chord at (a) as
the chromatic supertonic chord of C, and *quitting* it as the
dominant chord of G.

97. At (b) a return is made to the key of C by restoring the
F♮. Here the chord is taken as the tonic seventh of G, and
quitted as the dominant seventh of C. The chord at (c) should
be specially noticed. Though it is (as regards its notes) the same
chord seen at the second quaver of (a), it is not here the dominant
seventh of G. The student will learn later that it would be very
weak after making one modulation to G and then returning to C
to go back to G immediately. Therefore the chord at (c) is now
treated as a chromatic chord in C, as is seen by what follows
(*Harmony*, § 475). The F♯ in the melody two bars later is only
a chromatic passing note between G and F♮; but at (d) a
transient modulation (or "transition") to A minor is effected in a
different way, which we must now explain.

98. At first sight, there seems here to be no connecting link
between the two keys; for the preceding bar cannot be in
A minor, or it would have G♯; while that note does not belong
to the key of C at all. The fact is that we have here the very
common case of an implied enharmonic modulation. If for G♯
at (d) we substitute its enharmonic, A♭, it will be seen that the
chord is the last inversion of a dominant minor ninth in the key
of C. It is taken as such; then, by the enharmonic change to
G♯, the chord becomes the first inversion of a dominant minor
ninth in A minor, resolved on the tonic in the following chord.
When a modulation is thus made by means of an implied
enharmonic change, it is usual (though not invariable) to write the
chord, as here, in the notation of the key which is being
approached, and not of that which is being quitted. Lastly, the
return is made to C major by taking the chord at (e) as the
subdominant of A minor, and quitting it as supertonic of C.

99. Though no modulations are here made except to the
nearest related keys, this simple little theme is very instructive, for
it furnishes examples of all the most common methods of modulating. At (a) and (b) we see chords taken as chromatic in one
key, and quitted as diatonic in another; at (d) the modulation is
made by means of an implied enharmonic change; and at (e) the
chord used for modulation is diatonic in both keys.

100. We next give examples of simple modulations in minor
keys; and for our first illustration we choose the well-known
Allegretto from Beethoven's seventh symphony.

BEETHOVEN.   Symphony in A.

Beginning in A minor, the first modulation is made at (*a*) to the relative major, by taking the first chord of the bar as the tonic of A minor, and quitting it as the submediant of C.   The treatment of the F♯ at the end of the bar proves it to be here part of the chromatic supertonic chord of C, and not the leading note of G. At (*b*) the music modulates to E minor by a similar process to the last, the chord being taken as tonic of C and left as submediant of E minor.   At (*c*) we return to A by contradicting the D♯ of the preceding chord, which is thus seen to be taken as the dominant chord of E and quitted as the chromatic supertonic chord of A. Lastly at (*d*) we find the chord of A major taken as a tonic chord in that key (with only a *transient* modulation to the tonic major), and left as the chromatic major chord on the tonic of A minor, the treatment of the chord being according to the rule given in *Harmony*, § 470.

101. In the above example, the first modulation is, as usual (§ 82), to the key of the relative major.   In the following arrangement by Bach of one of the old chorals, we see a different order of modulation.

BACH.   Cantata, "Ach, ich sehe."

It is rare in a minor key to find the first modulation, as here, to
the major key of the minor seventh (the relative major of the
dominant minor). It is effected at (*a*) by means of the only
diatonic chord common to the two keys—the chord of A minor
being taken as tonic in that key, and left as the supertonic of
G major. From G major the modulation is made at (*b*) to its
relative minor by taking the chord as a submediant and quitting it
as a tonic—the converse of the process shown at § 100 (*a*) and (*b*).
At the cadence in E minor in the following bar, the Tierce de
Picardie is employed, so as to lead back more naturally to
A minor, in which key the next phrase begins. The modulations
at (*c*) and (*d*) to the relative major and back will be readily
understood by the student after what has been already said.

102. As most of the modulations we have been examining are
made by means of triads common to the two keys, we next have
to enquire what are the possibilities of modulation by means of
triads only. We first take the major triad.

103. Every major triad may be, as a diatonic chord, the tonic,
dominant, or subdominant of a major key, and the dominant or
submediant of a minor key. A little thought will show that by
considering the chord merely from these points of view we can
effect modulations between five keys, thus—

I. By taking the chord as a tonic and quitting it as a
dominant, we can modulate to the subdominant key, major or
minor.

At the * in both these examples the chord is taken as tonic, and
quitted as a dominant, bringing us at (*a*) to F major, and at (*b*) to
F minor.

104. II. Conversely, by taking any chord as a dominant, and
quitting it as a tonic, we can modulate to the key of the dominant
major.

Here we begin in F major at (a) and in F minor at (b), and in each case modulate through the same chord as before to the key of C major.

105. III. By taking a chord as a tonic and quitting it as a submediant, we can modulate to the key of the mediant minor.

IV. Conversely, by taking a chord as the submediant of a minor key, and quitting it as a tonic, we can modulate to the key of the submediant major.

106. V. By taking a chord as a subdominant and quitting it as a submediant, we can modulate from a major key to its relative minor.

VI. Conversely, we can modulate from a minor key to its relative major by quitting the submediant of the minor key as the subdominant of the major.

107. It is very important to notice that in all cases where a modulation is effected by means of a triad, as the triad is itself ambiguous, *the modulation needs to be confirmed*—that is, the triad must be followed by other chords which clearly establish the new key. It will be seen that we have done this in all the examples we have given.

108. If we now take the minor triads, we shall find that, like the major, they can also be diatonic in five keys; for a minor chord may be the supertonic, mediant, or submediant of a major key, or the tonic or subdominant of a minor key; and we can, so to speak, "ring the changes" between these keys with minor chords, in the same way as with major ones. After the full examples given of modulation by means of major triads, it will be unnecessary to give similar passages with minor chords. We shall continue our catalogue of modulations by means of these triads, and leave the student to make examples for himself similar to those given above. He must begin by defining the key he is leaving by means of its principal chords; he must then introduce his ambiguous chord, and conclude by confirming his new key. We now give some of the chief modulations to nearly related keys by means of minor triads.

109. VII. By quitting the supertonic chord of a major key as a tonic, we can modulate to the minor key of the supertonic (the relative minor of the subdominant).

VIII. By quitting a minor tonic chord as a supertonic, as at § 101 (*a*), we can modulate to the major key of the minor seventh (the relative major of the dominant minor).

IX. By quitting the submediant of a major key as a tonic, as at § 101 (*b*) (*d*), a modulation can be made to the key of the relative minor.

X. By the converse process—quitting a minor tonic as a submediant, as at § 101 (*c*)—we can modulate to the key of the relative major

XI. By quitting a minor tonic as a subdominant, we can modulate to the key of the dominant minor.

XII. By quitting a minor subdominant as a tonic, we can modulate to the key of the subdominant minor.

110. Though we have by no means exhausted the subject, we have here shown twelve different ways of modulating between all the nearly related keys by means of those triads only which are diatonic in both keys. We have also made these modulations as concisely as we could—that is, in the fewest possible chords. But with nearly related keys, in which there are three or four triads in common, these ambiguous chords can be used in succession, leaving a momentary uncertainty about the tonality, which is often of excellent effect. For example, if we wish to modulate from

C to A minor, instead of going by the "short cut" shown in § 106 (*a*), we can proceed more deliberately, thus—

Here the chords marked with a bracket in the third and fourth bars may be equally well regarded as submediant, subdominant, and supertonic in the key of C major, and as tonic, submediant, and subdominant in A minor; and the use of three or four ambiguous chords makes the modulation sound smoother and less sudden.

111. Hitherto we have only spoken of modulations between nearly related keys; but it is possible, by diatonic triads alone, to modulate to an unrelated key, as in the following fine example by Beethoven—

BEETHOVEN. Sonata in E flat, Op. 7.

Here the passage begins in D minor; the chord ✳ at the fifth bar is taken as the first inversion of the submediant chord of D minor, and quitted as the first inversion of the dominant of E flat, to which chord the seventh is added in the next bar, and the modulation is confirmed by its resolution on the tonic chord.

112. There still remain to notice other important modulations which can be effected by means of triads—especially *major* triads. We saw in § 103 that every major triad could be a diatonic chord in three major and two minor keys. But besides these, it can be a chromatic chord in several other keys. It may be the chromatic major tonic chord in a minor key (*Harmony*, § 469); it may be a chromatic chord on the minor second of either a major or minor key, or the fundamental chromatic chord on the supertonic, also in either a major or minor key; or, lastly, it may be the chromatic major chord on the flat submediant of a major key.

113. Now let the student stop to think for a moment what a large addition this gives him to his means of modulation. Take for instance the chord of C major. We have already seen that it belongs as a diatonic chord to the keys of C, G, and F major, and of F and E minor. But we now find that as a chromatic chord it can also belong to the keys of C minor, B flat major and minor, B natural major and minor, and E major. There are therefore no fewer than eleven of the twenty-four major and minor keys between any two of which a modulation is possible by means of this one chord. The chord may be diatonic in both keys, as we have already seen ; it may be diatonic in one of the two keys and chromatic in the other ; or it may be chromatic in both.

114. To show what is *possible* (not what is *advisable*), we will give a few examples of extreme modulations (*i.e.,* to very remote keys) made by means of this ambiguous aspect of a major triad.

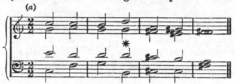

(a)

Here a modulation is made direct from C major to F sharp minor, by taking the fourth chord as the dominant in the former key, and quitting it as the Neapolitan sixth in the latter. So abrupt a modulation can rarely be made with good effect.

(b)

Here the modulation (from E major to B flat major) is still more unnatural, and is given only as an example of what is *possible*. It is effected by taking the chord ✻ as the chromatic chord on the flat submediant of E, and quitting it as the fundamental chromatic chord on the supertonic of B flat major. It will be seen that the chord is here chromatic in both keys.

115. While, however, such remote modulations as those here shown are extremely rare, we sometimes find this resource employed for modulations between keys that are in the second degree of relationship. We will first give a few simple progressions, illustrating such methods of modulating, and then quote some passages from the great masters in which these methods have actually been employed. To save space, we assume that the key we are quitting in each case has already been established, and give simply its tonic chord.

116. We take first the modulation from a major key to its
mediant major.   There are three triads by which this can be made.

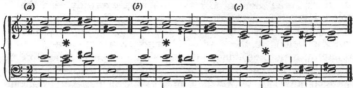

At (*a*) the tonic chord of the first key is quitted as the chord on
the flat submediant of the second ; at (*b*) the submediant of the
first key is quitted as the minor chord on the subdominant of the
second ; and at (*c*) the first inversion of the subdominant is quitted
as the Neapolitan sixth of the new key.

117. It should be noticed that the chord of modulation here
suggests in each case the key of E minor rather than of E major ;
indeed at § 105 (*a*) we used the same chord as here at (*a*) to
modulate from C to E minor ; and we could modulate to the same
key with the chords used at (*b*) and (*c*).   We shall find that in all
modulations between major keys in the second degree of relationship, when this is effected by means of triads, that these triads
will suggest a minor key which is related to both the major
keys

118. By a converse process to that just explained, we can
modulate to the key of the major third below—the flat submediant.

The student should have no difficulty in analyzing these modulations for himself.   Observe in the chords bracketed an illustration
of what has been said in the last section.   The chords at (*a*)
suggest an interrupted cadence in C minor, while at (*b*) and (*c*)
there are distinct suggestions of F minor.

119. In a similar way, we can modulate to the major keys of
the submediant and the flat mediant by means of triads which are
chromatic in the one key and diatonic in the other.   We give a few
simple examples, leaving the student to analyze them for himself.

(c)

Many more passages might by given, but these will suffice as illustrations; note again the suggestion of a *minor* key. The connexion between major and minor keys which are in the second degree of relationship to one another (§§ 87–90) is so natural and obvious, that no examples are necessary.

120. We now give a few quotations from the works of the great masters showing modulation by means of triads only, between keys which are in the second degree of relationship. Such examples are not very common; more frequently the modulation is effected by means of a discord.

MOZART. Jupiter Symphony.

In this well-known passage from the finale of the 'Jupiter' symphony, a modulation is made at * from G major to C minor by quitting the chromatic minor chord on the subdominant of the former key as the tonic of the latter.

121. Our next illustration shows the same chord used to effect a modulation to the major key of the mediant.

BEETHOVEN. Trio in B flat, Op. 97.

Here the chord * is taken as the submediant of F and quitted as the chromatic minor chord on the subdominant of A—the converse process of our last example, where the chord was taken as chromatic, and left as diatonic.

E

122. We next show the same chord used for modulating to the submediant—here from C to A major.

123. The following passage shows a modulation to the flat submediant—the key of the major third below—

Here the modulating chord is taken as a chromatic chord in F major, forming an interrupted cadence, and quitted as the tonic chord of D flat.

124. We have already incidentally referred (§ 111) to the possibility of modulating between unrelated keys by means of triads only, and shall now conclude this branch of our subject by giving some further examples of modulations of this kind, which are by no means uncommon. One of the chords frequently used for this purpose is the Neapolitan sixth—

Here a modulation from F sharp minor to C major is effected by taking the chord ✳ as the Neapolitan sixth in the former key and quitting it as the dominant of the latter. Compare the example § 114 (a).

125. In the following passage

SCHUBERT. Symphony in C, No. 7.

we see the chord ✳ taken as the tonic of B flat, and quitted as the Neapolitan sixth of A major

126. Our next examples show somewhat more unusual modulations.

Here the chord of E flat in the fourth bar is taken as the subdominant of B flat and quitted as the dominant of A flat.   It would have been more correct from this point of view that the passing note D should have been D flat; possibly Schubert thought of the modulation as being to E flat first, in which case we have here an example of "compound" modulation, which will be spoken of later.

127. The last illustration we shall give is very curious.

Here the chord ✽ is taken as the chromatic fundamental triad on the supertonic of B flat minor, and quitted as the tonic of C major. The ear expects a modulation to F minor at the third bar after the chord of C, and the effect of the sudden entry of the key of C major here is very striking.

128. We have dealt in this chapter exclusively with modulation by means of triads, and we have endeavoured to show how much is possible in this way alone.   But modulation by means of discords is perhaps even more common, especially in modern music ; and we enter here on another so wide a branch of our subject that we must devote a separate chapter to it.

CHAPTER VI.

THE MEANS OF MODULATION *(continued)*.

129. We have seen in the last chapter in how many different ways modulations can be effected by means of triads alone. We found it impossible to deal even with this branch of our subject exhaustively; and we shall be still less able to do so in treating in the present chapter of the many other methods of modulating which have still to be noticed. It may be confidently affirmed that the resources at the disposal of the musician are limitless, and that a composer of genius will be almost sure from time to time to discover some new device which has not previously been hit upon. All that can be done here is to indicate some of the chief methods of modulating, other than by triads, and to illustrate such methods from the works of the great composers.

130. We purposely in the last chapter excluded the diminished triad, because this is really the upper part of a fundamental discord; we now have first to show some of the modulations which can be effected by means of such discords.

131. Modulation by means of the fundamental chords of the seventh are not at all uncommon, especially between nearly related keys. Examples of these were seen and explained in the subject by Mozart given in § 96; they are often used, as there, in modulating between the keys of the tonic major and minor, the tonic and dominant, or the tonic and subdominant. Occasionally the same chord can be employed to bring together two unrelated keys, as in the following striking passage by Wagner—

WAGNER. 'Die Meistersinger.'

We have quoted enough of the context to show unequivocally that this passage begins in G. The chord in the third bar is therefore taken as the tonic seventh of that key; but its resolution proves that it is quitted, not (as usual in such a case) as the dominant of C, but as the supertonic of F, for the rest of the extract is unmistakably in that key. Every fundamental seventh evidently belongs to six possible keys, as it may be either dominant, supertonic, or tonic of a major or minor key, and for purposes of modulation it may be taken in any one of these keys and quitted in any other.

132. If the root of the chord of a fundamental seventh be omitted, we have the diminished triad. Evidently this form of the chord is also available for the modulations just mentioned. But in addition to these there is another modulation possible. The diminished triad on the supertonic of a minor key is the upper part, not of a fundamental seventh, but of a dominant minor ninth (*Harmony*, § 392); and by regarding such a triad in its two aspects it is possible to modulate from a major key to its relative minor, or *vice versa*. A good example of this is found in Mendelssohn's "Thanks be to God," in 'Elijah'—

MENDELSSOHN.   'Elijah.'

Here the chord ✳ is taken as the first inversion of the diminished triad on the leading note of E flat (second inversion of the dominant seventh of that key), and quitted as first inversion of the triad on the supertonic of C minor, which is really the third inversion of the dominant minor ninth in that key.

133. But it is not only the fundamental chords of the seventh that can be used for modulation; we can also employ the so-called "diatonic sevenths." In order to understand this clearly, it is important for the student to remember what was explained in *Harmony*, § 445,—that all these diatonic discords are in reality parts of the fundamental chord on the dominant. There are only

three possible forms of diatonic sevenths which are available for
the purpose of modulation. These are the following—

Of these the chord (a) with a major third, perfect fifth and major
seventh, is found on the tonic and subdominant of a major key,
and on the submediant of a minor key, and can therefore be used
for modulating between three keys; with the chord here shown
the keys would of course be C and G major, and E minor. The
chord (b) containing a minor third, perfect fifth, and minor
seventh, can be taken on the supertonic, mediant, and submediant
of a major key, and on the tonic and subdominant of a minor
key. It is therefore available for five keys. The chord (c), which
has a minor third, diminished fifth, and minor seventh, is met
with only on two notes—the leading-note of a major, and the
supertonic of a minor key. The only other forms of diatonic
seventh are the following, all of which belong to the minor key—

Of these (a) and (b) are useless for modulation, as they are found
on no other degree of the scale; the chord (c) will be treated of
later in this chapter (§ 139).

134. We now give a few examples of modulations by means
of these diatonic sevenths.

J. S. BACH.   ' Johannes Passion.

In this passage the quaver C in the bass is shown by the D in the
tenor to be an accented passing note. The modulation from A
to F sharp minor is therefore effected by taking the chord * as the
diatonic seventh on the supertonic of A,—in reality the second
inversion of the dominant eleventh—and quitting it as the seventh
on the subdominant (third inversion of the dominant thirteenth)
of F sharp minor.

135. Our next illustration shows the same modulation—from
a major key to its relative minor—differently managed, though
still with diatonic sevenths.

J S. BACH. Cantata, "Ich bin ein guter Hirt.

Here the chord ✳ is taken as a seventh on the subdominant of
E flat, and quitted as a seventh on the submediant of C minor.
In their harmonic origin these chords are respectively the third
inversion of the dominant thirteenth of E flat, and the fourth
inversion of the dominant thirteenth of C minor. Observe that,
though the details are different, the principle of procedure is the
same in this and in the preceding example. In both cases the
degree of the scale in the minor key on which the chord is seen
is a third higher than in the major key, while the generator is a
third lower.

136. Our next illustrations are more modern—

MENDELSSOHN. 'Elijah.'

Here a modulation is made from F sharp minor to D major by
taking the chord ✳ as the seventh on the subdominant of the
former key (third inversion of the dominant thirteenth), and
quitting it as seventh on the submediant (fourth inversion of
dominant thirteenth) in the latter.

137. We saw in §§ 134, 135 modulations from a major key to
its relative minor. We now show the converse modulation—from
a minor key to its relative major.

MENDELSSOHN. 'Athalie.

Here the modulating chord is taken as a diatonic seventh on the
supertonic of G minor (fourth inversion of a dominant eleventh),

and quitted as a seventh on the leading note of B flat (third inversion of the dominant major ninth).

138. In the passage just examined the modulation is effected by a dominant major ninth. The supertonic and tonic major ninths can also be used for modulation. It will be remembered that in the inversions of chords of the ninth the generator is mostly omitted (*Harmony*, § 370). In this case the chord will look like a chord of the seventh; but as the supertonic and tonic discords are always chromatic, we shall now have *chromatic* sevenths, and not diatonic as hitherto. One example of each will suffice.

(a)   MENDELSSOHN. Variations in E flat, Op. 82.

In this passage the chord ✱ is taken as the third inversion of the supertonic major ninth in E flat, and left as the fourth inversion of the dominant eleventh in G minor.

(b)   J. S. BACH.   Cantata,   O Ewigkeit, du Donnerwort."

Here the chord ✱ contains the same notes as the corresponding chord in the preceding example; but it is now taken as the third inversion of a tonic major ninth in F, and quitted, as before, as the fourth inversion of the dominant eleventh of G minor.

139. It will be obvious that fundamental chords of the minor ninth, like those of the seventh, can be used for modulation between six nearly related keys (§ 131). As a matter of fact they are not infrequently employed in this manner, as in the example given in *Harmony* at § 535. But the chief importance of this chord for the purpose now under consideration arises from the fact that its inversions, by means of *enharmonic* modulation, can belong to any one of the twenty-four major and minor keys. This point has been so fully explained in *Harmony* (§§ 542–544) that it will be sufficient to refer the student to what was there said, and to give a few examples from the works of the great masters, of enharmonic modulation by means of this chord.

140. Our first illustration shows a modulation from a minor key to its relative major.

The student already knows that this simple modulation might be effected in many other ways. Here the chord ✳ is taken as the third inversion of the supertonic minor ninth in G minor (of course with C♯), and quitted as the second inversion of the same chord in the key of B flat, the notation, as usual, being that of the key which is being approached, and not of that which is being left. The chord is resolved in the following bar on the root position of the dominant eleventh.

141. A specially fine example of modulation by this means is seen in the following passage :—

The modulation from the third to the fourth bar, in which there is apparently no chord common to the two keys of F minor and G minor, will be referred to later in this chapter (§ 145) ; the point for which the passage is quoted is the sudden modulation at ✳ from G minor to E minor, by taking the chord as the last inversion of a supertonic ninth (with B♮) in the former key, and quitting it as the first inversion of a supertonic ninth (with A♯) in the latter.

142. Spohr was very partial to this kind of enharmonic modulation; our next illustration is from his works.

SPOHR.   'Last Judgment.

Here, at the fourth and fifth chords, we see two minor ninths in succession; and the modulation might be considered as taking place on either of these.   If we regard it as taking place on the first, the second chord of the second bar is taken as the first inversion of a tonic ninth in G, and left as the third inversion of a dominant ninth (with C♭ and E♭♭) in G flat, being resolved on the first inversion of a supertonic ninth.   We prefer here to consider the modulation as being made at the chord *, because the preceding chord is not written in the notation of the key which is being approached.   The chord * is therefore taken (with F♯ and A♮) as the third inversion of the dominant minor ninth in G, and quitted as the first inversion of the supertonic minor ninth in G flat.

143. Our last example of this modulation brings together two very remote keys.

BEETHOVEN.   Sonata, Op. 26.

A modulation is here effected from D major to A flat minor by quitting the third inversion of the supertonic minor ninth in D as the first inversion of the same chord in A flat minor.   The student will readily see what enharmonic changes are required. In all the examples we have given, the chord of modulation is written in the notation of the new key; this is the general, though not the invariable, practice of composers.

144. While the chord of the minor ninth is probably that which is most frequently used in enharmonic modulation, it is not the only one available for this purpose.   The chord of the fundamental seventh, by an enharmonic change of its upper note becomes a chord of the augmented sixth, and *vice versa.*   It is

generally the dominant or tonic seventh which is thus treated, very seldom the supertonic, because this would connect two very remote keys (*e.g.*, C major or minor, and F sharp major or minor), and such a modulation can mostly be better managed in another way.   Evidently the only form of the chord of the augmented sixth which can be used here (at least in four-part harmony) is the *German* sixth; for the French sixth contains a note (the fourth) which is not part of a chord of the seventh, while the Italian sixth is inadmissible because of its doubled third.

145. Our first example of this modulation contains two or three matters for comment.

SCHUBERT.   Quintett, Op. 114.

To show the harmonic progressions more clearly, we have omitted the arpeggios for the piano, and given only the string parts of the passage.   The music commences in F major, the key of the movement; the second bar gives the third inversion of the tonic seventh of that key.   The chord in the third bar is not in the key of F, but looks like the dominant seventh of G minor; in fact the harmonic progression is identical with that by Handel which we saw in the third and fourth bars of the example to § 141. While, however, the chord of the seventh on D cannot belong to the key of F, the preceding chord can be in the key of G minor, and is, in fact, the upper part (seventh, ninth, eleventh, and thirteenth) of the chord of the tonic thirteenth in that key, resolved, quite according to rule, on a dominant discord.   In *Harmony*, § 575, will be found another example of the same form of this chord.

146. The second and third chords of the passage we are now analyzing therefore prove the key of G minor; but, as we are going to leave that key immediately, we have here another example of "compound modulation" (§ 159).   In the chord of the dominant seventh of G minor, C♯ is now enharmonically changed to B♯, and the chord becomes the German sixth on the submediant

of F sharp minor, in which key a full cadence is made, the last
chord of which it is needless to quote.   Observe here that the
modulating chord is written in the notation of the key quitted, no
doubt because the harmonic progression would have appeared
more obscure had a tonic seventh in the key of F been resolved
on an augmented sixth in the key of F sharp minor.

147. Our next illustration

SCHUBERT. 'Rosamunde.'

is somewhat similar to the last, except that there is no compound
modulation here, and that at ✳ the resolution of the augmented
sixth (really B♯) is delayed by an upward suspension.   It should
be noticed that when a dominant seventh is enharmonically
changed to an augmented sixth, the tonic of the new key will be a
semitone lower than that of the preceding ; also that the two
chords will be in the same position—that is, the root position of a
dominant seventh becomes the root position of a German sixth,
and the inversions will also be the same, as will be seen in our
next example.

148. We now show the converse case, in which a chord is
taken as a German sixth, and quitted as a dominant seventh

SCHUBERT. Symphony in C, No. 7.

This very fine passage will perhaps be found rather troublesome for the student to analyze, because of the extreme key (C flat major) in which it commences.   The chord of modulation would in C flat be written thus—

and, as the notation of nearly every note is enharmonically changed it becomes perplexing.   But if we remember that the enharmonic key of C flat is B natural, and write the passage from the third bar in that key, it becomes clear at once.

With this notation, the chord is at once seen to be the last inversion of the German sixth in B; by the enharmonic change it becomes the last inversion of the dominant seventh of C   An enharmonic change from an augmented sixth to a dominant seventh raises the tonic a semitone, just as we saw in the last section that the converse change lowered it to the same extent. We are of course speaking of the augmented sixth on the minor sixth of the scale; the much rarer chord on the minor second of the scale is seldom, if ever, changed in the same way, as the modulations thus induced would be very remote.

149. In our next example we see the tonic seventh, instead of the dominant, changed to an augmented sixth.

BEETHOVEN. Sonata, Op. 53.

This is a case of by no means infrequent occurrence; it obviously induces a modulation to the major or minor key of the mediant.

150. The last example to be given of this method of modulation differs in some respects from the preceding ones.

BEETHOVEN. Sonata, Op. 31, No. 3.

The key at the beginning of this passage is E flat, and the chord at the fourth bar must in that key contain G♭. In this shape it looks like the dominant seventh of D flat, but it is really the upper part of the dominant thirteenth of E flat. By the change to F♯ the chord becomes the augmented sixth in C minor, to which key a modulation is made. It is not uncommon for the upper part of a fundamental thirteenth to look like a complete chord of the fundamental seventh ; in the second bar of the example in § 145, we saw a chord regarded in both these aspects—as a seventh from F, and a thirteenth from G.

151. There is yet one more chord which can be used for enharmonic modulation. This is the chord of the minor thirteenth in its simplest form, with only generator, third and thirteenth present. By enharmonically changing any one of the notes of this chord it becomes another chord of the minor thirteenth, containing the same notes as before (generator, third, and thirteenth), but each in a different key, and in a different position.

Here the chord at (a) is the root position of the minor thirteenth on E, and, as a dominant, supertonic, or tonic chord, can belong to the keys of A, D, or E, major or minor. By changing G♯ to A♭, as at (b), the chord becomes the first inversion of a thirteenth on C, and can belong to the keys of F, B flat, or C, major or minor. If we further change E to F♭, as at (c), we have the last inversion of a thirteenth on A flat, belonging to six other keys. The chord (d) is, of course, only the chord (c) with every note enharmonically changed, and induces no new modulations.

152. Considering that by means of this chord we can modulate between eighteen different keys, it is perhaps strange that it is so seldom used. The following is a good example of its employment—

SCHUMANN. Intermezzo, Op. 4, No. 3.

The first four bars of this extract show an interesting sequence of diatonic ninths (*Harmony*, § 450) which is clearly in the key of C.

The chord at (*a*) is the tonic minor thirteenth on C, G♯ being written instead of A♭.   At (*b*) a modulation is made to the key of D flat by enharmonically changing E♮ to F♭ ; the chord then becomes the first inversion of a minor thirteenth on A♭.   The note is not written in the notation of the key which is being approached, because the minor thirteenth, when it resolves by rising a chromatic semitone, is usually written as an augmented fifth (*Harmony*, § 553).

153. As examples of modulation by means of this chord from the works of the great composers are scarce, we give a short passage written expressly to show all its possibilities.

In these eight bars the chord under notice is introduced six times. At (*a*) and (*b*) are the root position and first inversion of the chord on B, at (*c*) and (*d*) the last inversion of the same chord on G—the notation of (*d*) being disguised ; at (*e*) is the root position of the chord on E flat ; and lastly at (*f*) is the same chord as at (*b*), with the same treatment.   We will not analyze the modulations induced by these enharmonic changes, as it will be profitable for the student to do this for himself.

154. Hitherto all the modulations of which we have spoken have been effected by means of chords common to the two keys ; but we sometimes also meet with cases in which there appears to be no such connecting link.   These will almost always be in modulations between nearly related keys, the most common being from a major key to one of its three nearly related minor keys. We saw in the last chapter how to make such modulations by means of chords common to the two keys ; but it is often made by following a chord distinctly belonging to the one key by one no less distinctly belonging to the other, as in the following simple passages, in all of which, commencing in C, we assume that that key has been already established.

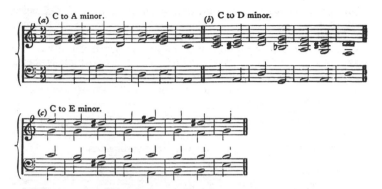

At (*a*) we follow the tonic chord of C by the dominant chord of
A minor, and at (*b*) by the dominant chord of D minor; while at
(*c*) the dominant chord of C is followed by the dominant chord of
E minor.   Observe that in every case the chromatic note foreign
to the key of C is the leading note of the new key, and that the
notes of the scale of C which are chromatically altered are the
tonic, dominant, and supertonic.   We can always make a modulation by sharpening one of these three notes of a key, to make it
into a leading note.   Obviously it would also be possible (though
less usual) to modulate into the tonic majors of the three minor
keys here shown by the same means.

155. It must be remarked here that it is *possible* here to
consider that there is a chord common to the two keys.   For
instance, at (*a*) of the last example, we might call the chord of C
major the upper part of the supertonic minor thirteenth of A
minor; while at (*b*) we might regard it as the upper part of the
tonic eleventh of D minor; and at (*c*) the chord of G might be
the upper part of a supertonic thirteenth in E minor.   Or, on the
other hand, by assuming an implied enharmonic change in the
dominant chords of the new key, we can bring all these chords
into the keys we are leaving, as various forms of thirteenths.   We
give these explanations to show the possibility of establishing a
connexion by means of chords common to the two keys; but it
must be admitted that it is rather far-fetched, and that the
principle laid down in the last section is much simpler and more
natural.

156. It will be noticed that in all the examples given in § 154,
the two chords where the modulation is effected have one note in
common.   At (*a*) and (*c*) the third of the first chord is the root of
the second, and at (*b*) it is the fifth of the second.   Sometimes a
modulation is made by retaining one of the notes of a chord
alone, and then taking it as a different note in the next chord.

F

The scherzo of Beethoven's seventh symphony affords a very fine example of this—

BEETHOVEN. Symphony in A.

Our extract is preceded by a full cadence in the key of F major. The third of this chord, after being sustained by itself for four bars, becomes the fifth of the chord of D major, with which the *assai meno presto* begins. It will be seen that the method of procedure is exactly the same as at § 154 (*a*), though the modulation is to the major, instead of to the minor, key of the submediant. It should also be noticed, that after the four bars of unison, *any* chord might have followed of which the note A formed a part.

157. But unison passages can also be used for modulation in other ways. A scale passage, whether diatonic or chromatic, can practically lead to almost any key; for it can stop on any note, and be followed by any chord to which that note belongs, or by a chord containing the next note of the scale above or below. Two passages by Schubert will illustrate this.

SCHUBERT. Sonata in A minor, Op. 164.

Here we twice see the ascending diatonic scale of A minor, each
time ending on the submediant of the key.   The first time there
is no modulation; but on the repetition of the passage, the note
F, taken as the submediant of A minor, is retained as the
dominant of B flat major, to which unrelated key a modulation
is made.   The modulation might also be considered as taking
place in the next bar (the chord being taken as Neapolitan sixth
in A minor, and quitted as tonic of B flat); but the explanation
we have just given seems here to be the more natural, because of
the analogy of the passage with that which follows the first scale.

158. An even finer example of a modulation by means of a
scale passage is the following—

Here we commence in F sharp minor, but at the *piano* in the fifth
bar begins a descending scale, chromatic after the first two notes,
and leading down to D♮.   This note is taken as the root of the
dominant seventh in G major, and followed by the passage quoted
in § 147.   The last note of that passage is immediately succeeded
by a repetition of the present one, with the substitution of C♯
for B as the first crotchet.   At the fifth bar Schubert now proceeds
as follows—

Here the chromatic scale ends a semitone higher than before, and
D♯, instead of D♮, is taken as the root of a dominant seventh,
bringing us most unexpectedly into the key of G sharp minor.
Observe that in each case the notes of the chromatic scale are

written in the correct notation of the key which is being approached.

159. Not infrequently, especially in modulations between unrelated or remote keys, some other key is incidentally touched upon in passing. In such a case the modulation is said to be *compound.* It is requisite for a compound modulation that there should be no confirmation of the intermediate key by means of a cadence in it—in other words, the incidental modulation must only be transient (§ 77). We have already seen one good example of compound modulation in § 145; we now give another, also by Schubert.

SCHUBERT.   Sonata in A minor, Op. 42.

Here the two very remote keys of A flat minor and E minor are connected in a manner as new and original as it is seen on analysis to be simple and natural. At ✳ there is an enharmonic change of notation (not modulation), the chord of G♯ minor being identical with that of A♭ minor. The chord is taken as a tonic, and quitted as the last inversion of a dominant major thirteenth in E major, resolving on the second inversion of the dominant seventh, which, in its turn, resolves on the tonic of E *minor.* Easy as such a modulation looks, it is in such unexpected strokes that the genius of a composer is revealed.

160. We saw in § 79 the importance of the motive in determining the point of modulation. The motive, as the smallest subdivision of a phrase or sentence, will always be in one key; and a modulation will always occur, not in the middle of a motive, but at the beginning of one. We remember that it requires at least two chords to make a modulation, just as at least two notes are necessary to form a motive; and, exactly as, in the latter, the second of the two notes must be the accented one, so the chord confirming a modulation should be on a more strongly accented beat (or bar, if there be only one accent in a bar) than the chord inducing it. If the student examines the various examples of modulation given in this and the last chapter, he will see this principle carried out in nearly every case.

161. We will now give a few passages illustrating some of the less frequent ways of modulating, but which cannot be classified under any of the heads we have given. Our first example is taken from the Adagio of Mozart's great quintett in G minor.

In order to show the part-writing clearly it has been necessary to use a compressed score of three staves. The score is more than ordinarily difficult to read, because Mozart, probably to make the separate parts easier to each player, has written some of them with sharps and some with flats. We therefore give the outline of the harmony with a notation which can be more easily followed.

162. Our quotation is immediately preceded by a full cadence in E flat minor, in which key therefore the passage begins. The chord at the end of the first bar is taken as the Neapolitan sixth in E flat minor, and quitted as the tonic of F flat (E♮) major. The addition in the bass of B♮ in the next bar gives us the second inversion of the tonic, followed at the half bar by the root position of the dominant with a 4 3 suspension. The third and fourth bars show us the dominant seventh of the same key, in root position and first inversion, with chromatic passing notes in the second violin and violoncello. In the fifth bar the dominant seventh of E (or F♭) is enharmonically changed to the augmented sixth in E flat minor, to which key a return is made. It would be possible

to consider that there is a transient modulation to F sharp minor in the third bar, and again in the fourth; but in such cases the passage must be looked at as a whole; and it is simpler and more natural to explain the notes, as we have done above, as chromatic passing notes, and to regard them as examples of *apparent*, and not real modulations.

163. Our next illustration

shows an unusual and very abrupt modulation from F major **to C** sharp minor. In order to see the connexion of the two keys **we** must think of the latter as D flat minor—the tonic minor of the flat submediant in F. The modulation is effected by taking the chord in the third bar as the first inversion of a dominant minor thirteenth in F, its notation in that key being

By an enharmonic modulation (changing E♮ to F♭) the interval of the diminished fourth from E to A♭, becomes a major third, and the chord becomes the tonic chord of the new key.

164. A somewhat similar modulation—now from D minor to C sharp minor—is seen in the following passage—

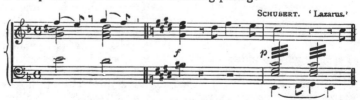

Here again we have an enharmonic modulation by means of a chord of the thirteenth. The first chord of the second bar cannot possibly belong to the key of D minor, because the E flat which it would then contain could only be derived from the tonic,

and **G sharp** only from the supertonic.   The chord of **modulation**
is therefore the **second** chord of the first bar, which in C **sharp**
minor will have E$\sharp$ instead of F$\natural$, and will be the fourth **inversion**
of the tonic thirteenth, with **third,** minor ninth, and minor thirteenth,
precisely the same form of thirteenth as in the last example—
resolving on a dominant discord.   The G in the upper part is, of
course, only an auxiliary note.   Observe that the chord **confirming**
the modulation is on a stronger accent than that inducing it (§ 160).

165. We next show a **very unusual** way of making a very **usual**
modulation—**to the key of the subdominant.**

WAGNER.   'Tristan und Isolde.'

We have numbered the fifth and tenth bars for convenience **of**
reference.   At the third bar we see the chord of the tonic minor

thirteenth in A flat, resolving in the next bar on the third inversion
of the supertonic eleventh (*Harmony*, § 552), the eleventh falling
to the third at the end of the bar.   In the fifth bar we have the
second inversion of the tonic ninth in D flat, the ninth falling to
the root in the next bar.   The chord of the seventh which remains
resolves on the supertonic ninth (over a dominant pedal) in the
seventh bar, and this in its turn on a dominant seventh (with an
appoggiatura) in the ninth bar.   In bar 10 the dominant seventh of
D flat is quitted as tonic seventh of A flat, resolving on the dominant
ninth of the same key.   The whole passage is a striking example
of that free use of chromatic harmony which is one of the most
characteristic features of 'Tristan und Isolde.'

166. Our last illustration is taken from the same work.

Wagner.   'Tristan und Isolde.

Here we see a very interesting example of a compound modulation—from G to B minor, passing through the key of F sharp
major.   First let the student notice that in the first six bars, in
spite of the numerous accidentals, the music never leaves the key
of G.   All the chromatic notes are either auxiliary notes or parts
of chromatic chords.   In the seventh bar there is an enharmonic
modulation ; the first chord would be, in the key of G,

that is, the third inversion of the dominant minor thirteenth, the
notes present being the third, seventh, minor ninth, and minor
thirteenth   By the enharmonic change of three out of the four
notes of the chord, it becomes the first inversion of the supertonic
major ninth in F♯, resolved in the next bar on the dominant
seventh of the same key (the D♮ at the end of the bar is a
chromatic passing note, and the A♮—more correctly G×—is an

auxiliary note of A♯). The chord of the dominant seventh of F♯ in the eighth bar is quitted as a supertonic seventh of B minor, resolving on the dominant seventh of that key.

167. We have given the above passage as one of our illustrations, not only because of its musical beauty, but because on a casual glance it looks a particularly hard nut to crack; and we wished to show that there are few, if any, passages in the works of the great masters which a little thought and patience will not enable us to analyze satisfactorily. The student who wishes to go more deeply into the subject of chromatic modulation will find in the score of 'Tristan und Isolde' an almost inexhaustible field for research.

168. In this and the preceding chapter, an endeavour has been made to explain as clearly and concisely as possible the chief means of modulation. The application of these means cannot be taught. It is impossible to lay down any rule as to when one method of modulating is preferable to another. In this, just as in the invention of melody, the student must exercise his own judgment and skill. The only advice we can give is, to use as much variety as possible. Enharmonic modulation, in particular, should be sparingly employed, as it soon gives monotony to the music, and mannerism to the style. Extreme chromatic harmony should, with very rare exceptions, be regarded as the flavouring, not as the principal ingredient of the musical repast.

169. The student should now write modulations between all possible major and minor keys, making each modulation in at least two or three different ways. He should begin with modulations between nearly related keys, first by means of triads only, then with discords, and lastly by means of enharmonic modulation. He should then take the keys in the second degree of relationship, and lastly the unrelated keys, and deal with them in the same way. He will also find it extremely useful to practise modulating at the piano. In order to do this with ease, it is essential that he should be perfectly familiar with the chords common to the two keys, always remembering that there are no two keys, however remote, which have not some chords, and even some triads in common. It may be well to give him a caution against too frequent modulation by means of the chord of the minor ninth (the diminished seventh), a very easy and therefore seductive way for an indolent pupil, but one which soon becomes wearisome, and, as we have said above of enharmonic modulation in general, gives monotony to the music.

CHAPTER VII.

THE CONSTRUCTION OF SIMPLE SENTENCES WITH

REGULAR RHYTHM.

170. The student who has thoroughly mastered the contents of the preceding chapters of this volume will now be in a position to begin to compose short musical phrases and sentences of regular rhythmical construction. For this purpose, he will not at present have to apply the whole of his acquired knowledge of modulation, because in such short and simple exercises as he is about to write, it will hardly ever be advisable to modulate beyond the most nearly related keys, and we might add it will never be expedient to modulate to an unrelated key. Such modulations are chiefly found in the larger forms of which nothing has as yet been said.

171. In Chapters II. and III. we analyzed musical sentences, and showed that they could be subdivided into phrases, sections, and motives. We shall now pursue the opposite method—the synthetical, and proceed to build up sentences from their component parts. For this purpose, we begin with the smallest part ; and our first question will be, What can be done with the motive?

172. The simplest possible form of the motive—what we may term the *typical* motive—was seen in § 59 to be found in the last two chords of a full cadence. For the present we are only going to concern ourselves with the melodic form of the motive ; we therefore start with the simple progression from leading-note to tonic as the germ which we are about to develop. The tonic will, of course be on the accented beat.

It is not necessary that the two notes be leading-note and tonic ; any two notes at the distance of a second from one another, and bearing the same relation as regards accent, will answer our purpose equally well.

173. There is a great deal more to be done with this little motive of two notes than the student might imagine at first sight ; we shall show presently that it is possible to construct complete musical sentences from it. In the first place, it can be repeated, either at the same or at a different pitch.

Here are a few of the very simplest effects to be obtained from this motive. At (a) is the repetition at the same pitch; at (b) it is repeated each time a second higher; at (c) a third higher; at (d) a third higher and a second lower alternately, and so on. The student can easily find many other variations.

174. But we can make further changes by varying the lengths of the notes of the motive. For instance, in (b) we may substitute two quavers for the unaccented crotchets, when the motive will appear in the following shape—

Or we may make the unaccented notes into quavers and the accented into dotted crotchets—

Or, again, we may put the passage into triple time—

If between the repeated notes we insert an auxiliary note, we obtain a new variation—

Note in this last example where the division of the motives is marked, and remember the reason (§ 59).

175. But we have not yet nearly exhausted the possibilities of this simple motive. It may also be inverted—a descending

second being substituted for an ascending one—and an almost
infinite variety of combination is possible of the inverted with the
direct form of the motive. We give a few examples, first of the
inverted form alone, and then of the inverted and direct forms
combined.

Compare (*a*) and (*b*) with (*e*) and (*f*) of § 173. The passages at
(*c*) and (*d*) show combinations of the two forms of the motive. It
will be seen that we could easily make countless other varieties.
Let the student experiment for himself, and see what new forms
he can obtain.

176. Besides such alterations of the time as were seen in § 174,
use can also be made of augmentation and diminution of the
whole motive; and these will open up an infinity of new combinations into which we cannot go here. Though we have, so to
speak, touched little more than the edge of our subject, we have
said enough to give an idea of what can be made even from
so apparently unpromising a motive as this.

177. We sometimes meet with an entire musical sentence
constructed from so simple a motive alone. The choral of which
we have analyzed the commencement in § 61, is made entirely
from the typical motive which we have been treating. So also is
the melody of the following chant, by Dr. Crotch—

It will be seen that the first half of this chant is made from the
inverted, and the second half from the direct form of the motive.
The apparent irregularity of the rhythm, with alternate phrases of
three and four bars, will be explained in the next chapter of this
volume.

178. A very beautiful example of a sentence constructed from this same motive is the following, by Beethoven—

BEETHOVEN.   Sonata, Op. 23.

This eight-bar sentence, modulating to the dominant, consists of two four-bar phrases, each motive being separated from the following by rests.   On the repetition of the passage, these rests are filled up by the same motive—

At the fourth and eight bars will be seen a fresh modification of the motive.   This is really an augmentation of an irregular kind ; instead of the notes being of double the length, they are of only the same length, but are divided by rests.

179. With motives consisting of more than two notes, a kind of variation often to be met with consists in the alteration of intervals between some of the notes.   A good example of this method will be seen in the following passage—

BEETHOVEN.   Trio in C minor, Op. 1, No. 3.

This example is instructive in more than one respect. The
motives here have mostly a feminine ending. This is proved by
the third,  in which the B ♮, being the resolution of the preceding C, must belong to the same motive, and
we therefore (§ 63) are able to determine the limits of the other
motives by analogy. (Compare the feminine ending in the
example from Bach, § 64.) In the first two bars of the present
passage, we see the repetition of the motive at the same pitch;
at the third is another repetition, but with the last note varied.
The next motive is inverted, and without the feminine ending.

180. The two following motives need no explanation; at the
seventh we see an entire change in the intervals, the quavers being
taken by leap instead of by step and only the rhythmical figure
(☐ ☐ | ☐ ☐)—very often spoken of as the rhythm—being pre-
served.* The last motive requires a little analysis, as, at first
sight, it does not seem to be the same as the others.

181. The harmony of the bar again proves a feminine ending
to the motive. To make the passage clear, we write out the turn
at full length—

If we think of the F and E as an ornamentation of the D,

we shall at once see that we have still the
same motive, though its form is somewhat disguised. The motive
now corresponds exactly to that which ends the first phrase; to
borrow an analogy from poetry, we may say that we have here a
musical *rhyme.*

182. Sometimes even greater modifications are found in the
form of a motive; it is, indeed, not uncommon to find only the
rhythmic figure (§ 180) retained. If this figure be strongly
marked, as in the passage last quoted, it will be sufficient to
establish the identity of the motive.

MOZART. Sonata in C.

p   *f*   *p*   *f*

(4)

* The word "rhythm" is often used in this sense, as well as in that in which we
have employed it in this volume. To avoid confusion, we shall use the term
"rhythmical figure," or simply "figure" to indicate the time-subdivisions of the
notes of a motive.

The feminine ending here is proved by the second and fourth
motives, while in the case of the third, its limits are defined by
the sudden change from *forte* to *piano* at the fourth quaver—
clearly showing the commencement of a fresh subdivision.
Similar considerations guide us in determining the limits of the
sixth motive, the end of which we see by analogy to be the third
quaver of the bar, as also appears from the *piano* after the G.
The last two motives of this sentence are quite new, but the first
six bars are evidently made from modified forms of the same
motive.

183. When a phrase or sentence is constructed from more
than one motive, it is desirable that these motives should be
contrasted, either in melodic outline, or in rhythmic figure, or in
both.   The following passage will illustrate this—

CHERUBINI.   'Anacreon.'

&c.

This sentence begins with three appearances of the same motive,
each time varied in its intervals (§ 179).   A new motive, with a
feminine ending, completes the fore-phrase with a half cadence.
The after-phrase begins with a fresh motive, also with a feminine
ending, as is proved by the rest with a pause in bar 6, which
follows its repetition.   At the beginning of the seventh bar we
see an incomplete motive—a point of departure (§ 60), followed
by a motive the dotted figure of which seems to have been
suggested by the commencement of the sentence.   The student
will observe that here each phrase divides into two sections.

184. We now proceed to show how to construct the simplest musical sentences, beginning with those of only eight bars in length. These are the shortest sentences which are generally to be met with in actual compositions; for, although we very frequently find sentences containing only four bars, these will almost always be found on examination to be bars of *compound* time, each of which contains two accents (§ 30). The first thing to remember is, that every sentence, in order to produce an effect of completeness, must be divisible into at least two phrases (§§ 24–26); otherwise the feeling of response and balance which is indispensable to the satisfaction of the mind will be wanting. From what has been said in the preceding chapters the student will know that these two phrases should be of equal length—that is of four bars each. It is hardly needful to add that the end of the first phrase will be shown by some kind of cadence.

185. A moment's consideration will show us something more concerning the sentence we are going to construct. We know that the cadence should always come in an accented bar; therefore the fourth and eighth bars of our sentence will be accented. Further, as the alternation of accent and non-accent should be regular, we see that the second and sixth will also be accented bars, though less strongly accented than the fourth and eighth, which respond to them; for we have already learned (§ 59) that response implies accent. In every regularly constructed sentence, therefore, the uneven bars will be unaccented, and the evenly numbered bars accented. If a sentence begin with an incomplete bar, then we begin to reckon from the following strong accent; and the first complete bar will be an unaccented bar. (See the examples in §§ 53, 56.)

186. The particular cadence to be chosen for the end of the fore-phrase is entirely optional If the sentence contain no modulation, the fore-phrase will most probably end with either a half cadence, or a full cadence with the third or fifth of the tonic chord at the top. It may also end with an inverted or interrupted cadence, or (more rarely) with a plagal cadence, or a plagal half-cadence, as in the example, § 30. If the sentence end with a modulation, the fore-phrase not infrequently contains a full cadence in the tonic key, with the root of the tonic chord in the upper part, as in the example by Haydn, in § 35 (*b*). If, on the other hand, the sentence closes in the tonic key, but the fore-phrase modulates, such modulation will generally be to a nearly related key—most usually the dominant for a sentence in a major, and to the relative major for a sentence in a minor key.

187. While we often find that each phrase of a sentence will divide into two sections, as in the examples in §§ 52, 56 and 72, it is also frequently desirable that one of the two phrases should so divide, while the other should be indivisible. In such a case it is

very common to make the second section a repetition, or imitation of the first.

HAYDN. Quartett, Op. 77, No. 5.

Here the fore-phrase divides into two sections, the second being a modified imitation of the first. The after-phrase begins with the same motive (with elided up-beat, and feminine ending) as the two sections of the fore-phrase, but the rest of the phrase is formed from an entirely new motive, and cannot be subdivided into sections. The construction of the sentence is

$$\overbrace{2+2}+4=8$$

Notice that here the fore-phrase ends with an inverted cadence.

188. It will be seen that this sentence naturally divides itself into three parts by means of the middle cadences. It will be convenient to adopt Dr. Riemann's plan of indicating these subdivisions by means of letters. The first theme of the sentence, two bars in length, we call A; the second, which is a variation of the first will be shown to be such by the addition of an asterisk; the second theme of the sentence (bars 5 to 8) we call B. On this method the form of the sentence appears as

$$\overbrace{A+A^*}+B.$$

The bracket indicates that the two short themes together form one phrase.

189. Our next illustration shows a very common form of sentence.

HAYDN. Quartett, Op. 64, No. 1.

(6)   (8)

The student will now be sufficiently accustomed to the analysis of
sentences to render it unnecessary to do more than mark the bars
in which the cadences, and therefore the subdivisions fall.   Here
each phrase divides into two sections ; the fore-phrase ends with a
half cadence.   The first section of the after-phrase is identical
with the corresponding section of the fore-phrase ; but the second
section is varied so as to lead to a full cadence.   Calling the two
sections, as before, A and B, the formula for a sentence of this
kind will be

$$\overparen{A+B}+\overparen{A+B}*$$

Examples of this form of sentence are almost continually to be
met with.   The opening of the theme of Beethoven's variations
in G is a very good specimen.

190. Another form hardly less common, and bearing much
resemblance to that just shown, is seen in the following passage—

W. S. BENNETT.   Overture, 'Paradise and the Peri.

(2)

(4)

(6)   (8)

Here again, each phrase divides into two sections; but, whereas the third section is, as in our last example, a repetition of the first, the fourth, instead of being a variation of the second, brings entirely new material. This fourth section we call C, and the formula for the sentence is

$$\widetilde{A + B} + \widetilde{A + C}.$$

191. In our next example

MOZART.   Sonata in E flat for Piano and Violin.

each phrase contains two sections; the first three sections are sequential in construction, while the fourth contains new material. Here we see the form

$$\widetilde{A + A} + \widetilde{A + B}.$$

192 It is somewhat less common to find the second section of the fore-phrase repeated as the first section of the after-phrase (either with or without transposition) as in the following—

MOZART.   Sonata for Piano and Violin in E minor.

Here the student will readily see that the formula is

$$\widetilde{A + B} + \widetilde{B + C}.$$

193. Space forbids us to discuss all the possible variations of this simple form. Before proceeding to speak of sentences that modulate, we give one example, again by Mozart, in which each of the four sections contains different material, the formula being, of course

$$\widetilde{A+B} + \widetilde{C+D}.$$

Mozart. Sonata in B flat for Piano and Violin.

194. We have already given in Chapter II. so many specimens of eight-bar sentences containing modulations (see §§ 32–35), that we need only supplement them here by a few examples of the less frequent varieties. Our first shows the not very common case of a sentence which modulates to the key of the relative minor.

Beethoven. Variations, Op. 76.

Here we have another example of the form

$$\widetilde{A+B} + \widetilde{A+B}*$$

195. The modulation from a major key to the major key of the submediant (a key in the second degree of relationship) is also somewhat rare.

BEETHOVEN.   Bagatelles, Op. 33, No. 3.

The formula of this sentence is evidently the same as the last. Another good example of this modulation (but in a sentence sixteen bars in length, and differently constructed) will be seen at the beginning of the scherzo of Beethoven's Pastoral Symphony.

196. Our next two illustrations are counterparts of one another.

HAYDN.   Quartett, Op. 6, No. 2.

Here the fore-phrase ends in the tonic key, with an inverted cadence ; the sentence modulates from D minor to the major key of its dominant.   It will be seen that it is now the second section, and not the third, which corresponds to the first, and that the form of this sentence is

$$\widetilde{A + A} + \widetilde{B + B}$$

197. In the following passage we see the converse case ; the fore-phrase now ends in the dominant major, and the after-phrase

returns to the tonic key. Observe that the four bars of compound time are equivalent to the eight bars of the preceding examples.

198. We next give an example of a modulation from a minor key to its tonic major.

In spite of the close connection of these two keys in their harmonic derivation, this modulation is much less frequent than that between relative major and minor keys. Of the great composers, Schubert has probably been the one who has employed it most frequently.

199. We said in § 170 that in short sentences it was never expedient to modulate to an unrelated key. The following passage may be regarded as the exception that proves the rule—

Here the very abrupt modulation from B major to C major at the fifth bar, though effective enough as Schubert has introduced it, can hardly be recommended as a model for general imitation.

200. It is but seldom that we meet with a complete composition containing only one sentence of eight bars. The following little song, from Schumann's 'Lieder-Album für Jugend,' is therefore worth giving as a rare example—

SCHUMANN. 'Der Abendstern,' Op. 79, No. 1.

It will be seen that the fore-phrase ends with a half cadence in the relative minor.

201. The student may now begin to write eight-bar sentences in various forms for himself. He should first make them without modulation, writing them in minor as well as in major keys. He must remember in all cases to divide his sentence into two phrases at the fourth bar, by means of a middle cadence. One or both of the phrases should be subdivided into sections. If only one be so divided, the sentence will probably have the form seen in § 188,

$$\overbrace{A+A}+B$$

in which the second section will either be identical with, or similar to the first. It would also be possible (though less usual) to divide the after-phrase, giving a form

$$A+\overbrace{B+B}$$

But it is not necessary that the two sections be constructed from the same material : the following form is also available—

$$\overbrace{A+B}+C$$

202. As models for the student, we now write a simple sentence in each of these forms, varying the time and rhythmic figure in every case.

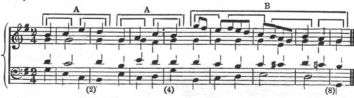

This sentence requires little explanation. We have marked the motives as well as the larger divisions of the music. It will be seen that it is mostly built up from our "typical motive" (§ 172).

203. In our next sentence we divide the after-phrase into sections, instead of the fore-phrase.

Here we have begun with a complete bar, to show the student that sentences can be so commenced. The first motive is therefore incomplete, its unaccented notes being elided (§ 60). We have already mentioned that the first bar will be an unaccented one (§ 185); this is always the case in a regularly formed sentence beginning with a complete bar. The fore-phrase has a feminine ending (compare § 63); and the similarity of the two sections of the after-phrase is obvious.

204. The following sentence has each portion formed from different motives—

As our last examples were in four-part harmony, we have written this sentence for the piano, for which much greater freedom of part-writing is allowed. We have also, for the sake of variety, concluded the fore-phrase with an interrupted cadence.

205. In our example of the last form mentioned in § 201,

we have indicated the time as *presto* to prevent any feeling of a second accent in the bar.   In a slow tempo this passage would be equivalent to a sixteen-bar sentence.

206. Although, in the different sentences given here as examples, we have marked the subdivision into motives, as well as into phrases and sections, it will be well to say that it is neither necessary nor expedient for the student, in writing similar sentences, to build them up laboriously a motive at a time.   Such a method would be like an author's constructing his sentences painfully word by word.   We wrote the sentence in § 202 in this way, because that was designed to illustrate the formation of a sentence from only one motive ; for it will be seen that the quaver figure at B is the diminution of the motive at A.   But in actual composition it is far more likely that a whole phrase, or at least a section (sometimes even a whole sentence), will be invented at once.   This was the case in the rest of our examples ; and the subdivision into motives was made afterwards.   The motive will be taken as the basis, when it is intended to develop a whole phrase from one germ.

207. Having written sentences in which only one of the phrases is divided into sections, the student should write others in which each phrase is so divided.   He can now also begin to introduce modulations, either at the end of the fore-phrase or at the end of the sentence.   The sentences can take any of the following forms—others are also possible.

$$\widetilde{A} + A + \widetilde{A} + B$$

$$\widetilde{A} + A + \widetilde{B} + B$$

$$\widetilde{A} + B + \widetilde{A} + B$$

$$\widetilde{A} + B + \widetilde{A} + C$$

$$\widetilde{A} + B + \widetilde{B} + C$$

$$\widetilde{A} + B + \widetilde{C} + D.$$

Where the same section is repeated, the repetition will frequently be varied, either in melodic outline, in harmony, in key, or in any combination of these.   After the numerous examples of these forms that have already been given, it is needless to write further illustrative sentences.   Those that we wrote in §§ 202–205 will sufficiently show the student how to set to work.

208. In the first chapter of this volume we referred (§ 13) to the close connection between melody and harmony.   This must never be lost sight of in constructing such sentences as those of which we are now speaking.   In this matter there is a most important rule to be given to the student.   With few exceptions,

such as a passage founded upon one chord, as, for instance, the
following—

BEETHOVEN. Sonata, Op. 22.

*the harmony should always be changed on an accented beat; and the
stronger the accent, the more advisable it becomes to change the
harmony.* We know that in the eight-bar sentences which we
have been constructing, the most strongly accented bars are the
fourth and eighth, and next to them the second and sixth. On
these bars we nearly always find a change of harmony; but it is
not at all uncommon to find the harmony of an accented bar
continued through the following unaccented bar. A very good
example of this will be seen in the passage from Bennett given in
§ 190. Here the cadence in F major at the fifth bar clearly shows
the end of a phrase—in other words, an accented bar; and the
harmony of this bar is repeated in the following (unaccented) bar.
The same principle applies, if there is more than one chord in a
bar, to the smaller subdivisions. In the simplest form of motive,
containing only one unaccented and one accented note (see our
example § 202) we mostly find a new harmony on the accented
note of the motive, as in the first four bars of this example;
though the same harmony, or at least the same bass note, is often
continued to the unaccented part of the following motive. This
is seen in bars 6 and 7 of the same example.

209. The student must not infer from what has been said that
it is always wrong to anticipate the harmony of an accented bar
or beat on the preceding unaccented; but it must be pointed out
that when this is done—and it is by no means infrequent in
modern music—the effect will be produced either of an anticipation or of a syncopation, which is nearly the same. This will be
seen from the following passages—

BEETHOVEN. Piano Trio, Op. 1, No. 2.

In the first of these passages we have marked the motives, as there is only one accent in a bar, and the motives are here two bars in length (§ 70). The anticipation of the harmony in the last four bars will be clearly felt. A very similar effect, though more pronounced, is produced in the extract from Schumann's sonata.

210. Sentences of twelve bars' length, and containing three four-bar phrases, though far less common than those of eight or sixteen bars, are sometimes to be met with. The commencement of the air, "Voi che sapete," in Mozart's 'Figaro' (quoted in § 14), is an example of such a sentence, and another will be seen in § 43. In both these passages each phrase is constructed of different material. Using letters, as before, the formula for these sentences will be

$$A + B + C.$$

We give another example of a sentence similarly formed.

There is one difference to be noticed between this sentence and those just referred to. Here each phrase has the same rhythmical figure, though the melody and harmony are different in all three.

211. More commonly, however, when a sentence is composed of three four-bar phrases, it will be found that either the first and second or the second and third phrases are nearly if not quite the same. A few examples will make this clear.

HAYDN. Symphony in C.

The first and second phrases here have feminine endings, and are virtually identical, the cadence alone being slightly varied. The third phrase ends with a modulation to the dominant. The formula of this sentence will be

$$A + A + B.$$

212. Our next illustration is somewhat different.

BEETHOVEN. Sonata, Op. 2, No. 1.

Here the second phrase is a transposition of the first into the key of the relative major; each of these phrases divides into two sections. The third phrase also contains two sections, the first of which is the same as the second section of the second phrase, with inversion of the two upper parts. Our formula for this sentence will therefore be rather more complex, as we must take note of the sections as well as of the phrases. It will be

$$\widetilde{A + B} + \widetilde{A + B} + \widetilde{B} + C.$$

213. By comparing our last example with the original text, it
will be seen that we have omitted the last two bars, in which the
final cadence is repeated.   We shall see in the next chapter that
such repetitions of cadences do not affect the real rhythmic
construction of the sentences.

214. It is probably quite as common to find the second phrase
repeated as the first.   In this case the second phrase will mostly
end with either an inverted or an interrupted cadence, which in
the third is changed to a full cadence.   The following passage is
a very good illustration of this—

Here the second phrase ends with what would be the usual form
of interrupted cadence were not the bass note at the end of the
seventh bar B♯ instead of B♮.   This change induces a transient
modulation to the key of the relative minor.   The formula for the
sentence is evidently

$$A + B + B.$$

215. Our last three illustrations have all been taken from
minuets.   It will perhaps be hardly too much to say that twelve-
bar sentences are more frequently met with in minuets than in
other forms, especially when these sentences are constructed on
either of the models A + A + B or A + B + B.   It is indeed a
question whether such passages as these should be regarded as
genuine twelve-bar sentences, or as extensions of an eight-bar
sentence (as we shall show in the next chapter) by the repetition
of one of its phrases.   In the case of sentences such as those

in §§ 43, 210, no such question can, of course, arise. Here there can be no doubt.*

216. Sentences of sixteen bars (§§ 44–47) so closely resemble those of eight bars in their general form and construction, that after the full directions given concerning the latter, not much need now be added. Any of the formulæ given in § 207 can be used in making these sentences, but the student must remember that each of the subdivisions will now be a phrase of four bars, instead of a section of two. He must endeavour to combine symmetry and variety, and must be especially careful to avoid monotony in his cadences. Beyond these general directions, no new instructions need be given.

217. We now give two examples of sixteen-bar sentences, both of which show points not illustrated in the sentences of the same length given in Chapter II.

MOZART. ' Così fan tutte.'

Here we have a sentence symmetrically divided into four four-bar phrases. Of these the first and third are identical, but while the second ends with a half cadence, the fourth ends with a full cadence. The form is therefore exactly the same as that of the eight-bar sentence given in § 189.

* Even in these cases, it is often preferable to regard a twelve-bar sentence as an extension of one of eight bars, as will be seen by the examples in the next chapter to §§ 234, 279.

218. Our second example is rather more complex.

MENDELSSOHN. Overture to 'Melusina.

Here the subdivision into four-bar phrases is much less distinct; for the first and second phrases, instead of containing a distinct middle cadence, as usual, end on a discord (compare the sentence

from 'Lohengrin' in § 47). After the inverted cadence in D flat
at the second bar, there is no point of repose till the twelfth bar,
where we find another inverted cadence. The first eight bars can
hardly be said to form two phrases ; for the seventh and eighth
bars are a repetition of the fifth and sixth, which are themselves a
variation of the third and fourth. We have here, in fact, on a
larger scale a similar form to that seen in the eight-bar sentences
in §§ 203 and 205, in which the fore-phrase was undivided, and
the after-phrase was divided into two sections. The formula for
this passage will therefore also be

$$A + \overset{\frown}{B + B}$$

with the difference that A now contains eight bars and B four.

219. This passage furnishes a very excellent example of the
way in which, in the larger musical forms, a sentence may be
extended and prolonged. If, by the omission of all repetitions,
we reduce the melody to its simplest form, it takes the following
shape—

It will be seen that we have here a perfectly regular eight-bar
sentence, constructed on the formula

$$\overset{\frown}{A + A^*} + \overset{\frown}{B + B^*}$$

By repetitions, with variations and prolongation of the passage
marked (*a*), the first four-bar phrase is extended to eight ; and the
repetition of the entire second phrase, with avoidance the first time
of the full cadence, completes the sixteen-bar sentence, of which
the two halves are now perfectly balanced.

220. It is impossible within the limits of such a volume as this
to deal with the numberless variations of detail to be found in
even such simple and regular sentences as those of which we have
treated in this chapter. All that is in our power is to indicate
general principles, and to show, as far as we can, what are the
fundamental laws underlying the construction of musical phrases
and sentences. We have several times had occasion to point out
that the eight- and sixteen-bar sentence is the *normal* one, and
that it is so because the balance and counterpoise of the members
of a sentence is a law of nature (§ 26). We have also shown the
importance of contrast as well of symmetry. If the student has
thoroughly grasped the principles already laid down, he ought now
to be able to construct regular sixteen-bar sentences for himself.

after the various models given for his guidance in this and preceding chapters.   How much musical value his exercises may
possess will depend upon the amount of imagination with which
he has been endued ; but even if his own compositions should be
worthless, the knowledge he has acquired will be of much value to
him in enabling him to analyze and to appreciate the works of the
great masters.   He is not, however, to suppose that he will always
find sentences as regular and simple in construction as those of
which we have been speaking.   These are mostly to be found in
smaller forms of composition, both vocal and instrumental.   Such
are many national airs and hymn-tunes, as well as much dance-
music.   But in the larger forms, more especially of instrumental
music, we meet with extensive modifications of these simple outlines ; and with these we shall proceed to deal in our next chapter.
It was necessary that the normal form should be thoroughly
understood before we could enter upon the important subject of
its variations.

H

CHAPTER VIII

IRREGULAR AND COMPLEX RHYTHMS.

221. Though the perfectly symmetrical four- and eight-bar phrases and sentences with which we have been dealing in the last chapter may be truly said to be the basis of all musical forms, it is only in smaller pieces that we find them uniformly and persistently maintained. In larger compositions, in order to prevent the monotony which would inevitably result were a cadence introduced at every fourth bar, we frequently find the sentences and phrases modified, sometimes by extension, sometimes by contraction. We have now to show how both these processes may be applied without disturbing the balance and proportion of the work. It will be most important for the student to bear in mind that the rhythms of which we have now to treat are not **actual** new forms, but *in every case variations of the normal rhythm of four and eight bars.* We shall first speak of those sentences in which extensions are made by the insertion of one or more bars, and then of those in which we find contractions, by the elision of bars or overlapping of phrases.

222. One of the simplest, and perhaps the most common method of extending a sentence is by *the prolongation or repetition of its final cadence.* The effect of a perfect cadence is that of repose, and the feeling is only strengthened if a pause be made upon the last chord, as is frequently done at the end of a piece. The same effect is produced if the final chord be repeated once or more, as in the following very familiar form of full cadence

Here we mark the bar in which the last chord of the cadence is found as (8) ; the following bars, containing the repetitions of the final chord, we indicate as (8a) and (8b), as they do not begin another sentence. We shall adopt the same plan throughout this chapter, whenever a bar is repeated.

223. But it is also possible, and not uncommon, to lengthen
the last chords of a cadence, thus making four bars into five,
without disturbing the cadential effect or the feeling of the balance
of the sentence. Let the student compare the two following
passages, quoted from the second volume of Marx's 'Composition'—

The example (*a*) is a regularly constructed eight-bar sentence,
divided into two phrases of four bars each. At (*b*) is a variation
of the same sentence, with the seventh bar extended into two.
We do not mark the second of these bars as (8), because this
would show the end of the sentence, which is not till the following
bar. The point which these passages illustrate is, that while the
feeling of the regularity of rhythm is is one sense disturbed by this
prolongation of the cadence, the effect is not unsatisfactory,
because the cadential second inversion at bar 7 naturally leads
the ear to expect the dominant chord to follow ; the cadence is
fully expected, and when it is reached it gives, perhaps, all the
more satisfaction from having been deferred. The repetitions of
the final chord illustrate what was said in the last section.

224. In our next example the prolongation begins rather
sooner.

MOZART.   Aria, " Per pietà, non ricercate."

As we quote here only the after-phrase of a sentence, we begin to
count the bars from 5 to 8. The sixth and eighth are, of course,

the accented bars. Up to the eighth bar, the form is regular,
being that which has been so often seen in the last chapter. At
bar 8 the sentence is prolonged by the substitution of an interrupted for a full cadence. The last two bars are then repeated in
a varied form, bar 7 being now extended into two. The prolongation of the cadence here only makes the feeling of repose
more complete.

225. It will be seen that the interrupted cadence is marked
(8 = 6). As we shall frequently in the course of this chapter have
occasion to use this and similar signs, it is important that its exact
meaning should be clearly understood. As the fourth bar of the
after-phrase, it is evidently (8); but as this eighth bar does not
here complete the sentence, it has a double function. The final
cadence at the end of the passage will be (8); obviously the next
preceding *accented* bar will be (6). The two bars which follow
are both unaccented, for they are merely (as said just now) an
extension of the unaccented bar (7); therefore the cadential bar
here is marked as the eighth in its relation to what precedes, and
as the sixth in its relation to what is to follow.

226. The above passage also illustrates two other important
points, with both of which we shall have to deal ;—the repetition
of an entire cadence, and the occurrence of two unaccented bars
between two accented. We shall first give examples of repetitions
and extensions of cadences.

227. In the following interesting passage

which is the conclusion of the scherzo of one of the best-known of
Beethoven's sonatas for piano and violin, we have, for the sake of
clearness, omitted the imitations in the violin part, as they do not
affect the construction of the sentence. As in our last example,
we have quoted here only the after-phrase. At the eighth bar is a
cadence with a feminine ending (§ 28) repeated without alteration

in the following bar (8a), and then again repeated, with extension over two bars—a kind of free augmentation.

228. Sometimes a cadence will be varied on its repetition.

HAYDN. Quartett, Op. 74, No. 2.

Haydn's 83 Quartetts are an exhaustless mine of varied rhythms, the study of which may be warmly recommended to all musicians who have access to them.   In the present passage we see a perfectly regular eight-bar sentence, ending with a half cadence (feminine ending) ; this is immediately succeeded by a full cadence in the dominant key (8a) on a tonic pedal ; this cadence is twice repeated in the two next bars, and followed by two repetitions of the tonic chord.   It will be noticed that the prolongations of the cadence themselves occupy four bars, so that there is a symmetry about the whole sentence, which consists of 4 + 4 (+ 4) bars.

229. Not infrequently, the fore-phrase, as well as the after-phrase, has a cadential prolongation.

HAYDN. Quartett, Op. 71, No. 3.

Here the bass notes of the cadence are repeated in unison as a kind of echo. The substitution of G for E flat in the final bar is probably due to the fact of the latter note being below the compass of· the violin.

230. Other kinds of variation of the extended cadence will be seen in our next examples.

Here there is an inverted cadence at the fourth bar, but it is quite evident from the structure of the passage that the two following bars, ending with a half cadence, belong to the fore-phrase. The fourth bar therefore must be regarded in a double aspect, like the eighth bar in our example, § 224 ; we accordingly mark it as $(4=2)$. The student will see that a four-bar phrase could begin in the third bar—

The after-phrase corresponds exactly in construction to the fore-phrase ; we therefore mark $(8=6)$, and the whole sentence is perfectly symmetrical, and in six-bar rhythm.

231. In the following passage

the eighth bar cannot conclude the sentence, as it has only an
inverted cadence with a feminine ending.   Here the $(8 = 6)$ construction is even more obvious than in the last example.   It will
be seen that here again the last four bars of the passage form a
perfectly satisfactory phrase.

232. Sometimes, though far less frequently, the commencement of a phrase or sentence is prolonged, instead of the end.
The following is a good example of this procedure—

MOZART.   Quartett, No. 23.

Here the first bar of each phrase is extended into two, just as we
saw was the case with the seventh bar in our examples, §§ 223 (*b*)
and 224.   Consequently we have in this passage an example of
five-bar rhythm.

233. In addition to such extensions as have been already
noticed, it is possible, and by no means uncommon, to interpolate
one or more bars *in the middle* of a sentence.   Sometimes one of
the sections will be repeated, as in the following passage—

MOZART.   Symphony in C, No. 36.

It is self-evident here that the first section of the after-phrase is repeated; no further explanation of the passage will be required.

234. Somewhat similar, but more extended, is the following example from Mendelssohn's 'Lieder ohne Worte.' To save space we give only the melody, because the music is in everybody's hands, and it is therefore unnecessary to quote the harmony, to which the student can refer for himself.

MENDELSSOHN.   'Lieder ohne Worte, Book 2, No. 4.

The first bar, which we have not quoted, merely establishes the figure of accompaniment, and, as we shall see presently (§ 265), does not count as part of the first sentence. The first eight bars of the melody are perfectly regular; the harmony shows us by the position of the cadences which are the accented bars (§ 39). This sentence ends in F sharp minor, the A being sharpened to bring back the original key.

235. The second sentence is very greatly prolonged. The fore-phrase ends in the fourth bar with an inverted cadence in F sharp minor; the two-bar section which follows is first repeated exactly (6a), and then twice in a varied form (6b and 6c). It is perfectly clear that neither of these points marks the close of the sentence; for a sentence cannot end on a second inversion. The fact that each of these two-bar sections is not only built on the same motive, but (what is more important here) ends on the same $\frac{6}{4}$ chord, shows each of these accented bars to be a repetition

of (6) ; we therefore mark them (6a, b, c). When at last the cadence is reached, at the *ff*, instead of the expected full close in F sharp minor, we have an interrupted cadence, inducing a modulation into D major. This bar, therefore, though final in its relation to what has preceded, leads into the passage that follows. If this passage were merely a repetition or emphasizing of the cadence, we should mark the following cadence as (8a). (Compare the cadences in the examples, §§ 227, 228.) We have not done so here, because a new after-phrase is added ; the phrase ending with the interrupted cadence is therefore not only the after-phrase to its predecessor, but the fore-phrase to that which follows. For this reason we mark it (8 = 4).

236. We have two reasons for not regarding the eight bars that follow as forming a new sentence. First, as we have already explained, the interrupted cadence shows that the last sentence is not completed ; besides this, of the eight next bars the second four are only a repetition of the first with a varied cadence. We therefore consider the bar with the full cadence in D as (8), and the following (inverted plagal) cadence in G as (8a). The repetition of the final cadence of course gives us (8b).

237. Here let us digress for a little, to prevent a possible misapprehension on the part of the student. We do not intend for a moment to assert, or even to imply, that a composer, when writing a sentence of irregular rhythm, such as those we are explaining in this chapter, is *consciously* making variations from the normal four or eight-bar sentence, any more than we should imagine that in inventing some new harmonic progression he troubles himself to think about the roots of his chords. But just as the theorist can satisfactorily explain any harmony the effect of which is good, even though the composer might quite possibly be unable to account for it himself, so we are endeavouring to show that the irregularities of rhythmical structure so frequently met with in the works of the great masters can be justified on intelligible grounds, if we only have some rational system on which to work. It would be absurd to imagine that Mendelssohn when composing the passage that we have been analyzing said to himself, "Now I will take an eight-bar sentence, and extend it by various means to twenty-four bars." He was doubtless guided by his musical feeling ; and the business of the theorist is to explain the principles on which, even unconsciously to himself, a composer works, and to show that his practice rests on a solid foundation.

238. We have now to deal with the numerous cases in which a phrase or sentence is lengthened by the insertion of one bar. Sometimes it is an unaccented bar that is interpolated, as in our example, § 224, two consecutive unaccented bars being thus brought between two accented. We have already seen an addi-

tional unaccented bar at the beginning of a phrase in § 232 ; we
now show its insertion in the middle of the phrase.

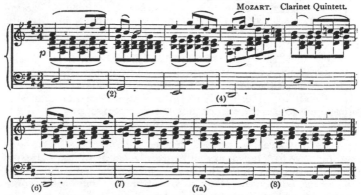

MOZART.   Clarinet Quintett.

Here the half cadence is deferred by the insertion of the unaccented bar (7a).   No further explanation is required.

239. Another very good example of this procedure is seen in
the first of Mendelssohn's 'Lieder ohne Worte.'   As in § 234, we
quote only the melody, leaving the student to examine the
harmony for himself.

MENDELSSOHN.   'Lieder ohne Worte, Book 1, No. 1.

Here the inserted bar (7a) is not a continuation, as in our last
example, but an actual repetition of the preceding bar (7).   The
following bar contains a cadence with a feminine ending ; as this
does not terminate the sentence, but leads to another phrase of
four bars, we mark it (8 = 4), as in the example in § 234.

240. Sometimes an unaccented bar is interpolated in both
phrases of a sentence, producing a regular five-bar rhythm, as in
the following passage—

SCHUBERT.   Sonata in E flat, Op. 122.

241. We generally find that when an unaccented bar is interpolated, it will be in approaching a cadence. This is the case in all the examples we have given: the additional bar will therefore mostly be either (3a) or (7a).

242. Far more common than the interpolation of an unaccented, is that of an accented bar. When only one such bar is introduced in a musical sentence, it will almost invariably be in the after-phrase, not in the fore-phrase; it is, indeed, extremely rare to meet with an instance of the latter.* The reason is obvious; the after-phrase (the *responsive* phrase) is by reason of its position, the weightier (§ 50). By adding to its weight, we disturb the natural balance of the sentence less than by putting an additional accented bar into the fore-phrase, which would make it, so to speak, "top-heavy"; for it would then contain three accented bars against two in the after-phrase. In the following passage

HAYDN. Quartett, Op. 55, No. 1

* The only instance we can remember to have met with of the addition of an accented bar to the fore-phrase of a sentence, and not to the after-phrase, is at the beginning of the Coronation March in Meyerbeer's 'Prophète.'

the position of the accented bars in the fore-phrase is self-evident; the sixth bar, being the repetition of the second, is clearly an accented bar.   The addition of G♮ to the chord changes it from the tonic chord of A to the dominant seventh of D; the following bar completes the cadence in that key; and, as the last chord of a cadence always falls in an accented bar (except occasionally with a feminine ending, which is not found here), the additional bar is clearly an accented one, and we mark it (6a).

243. Our next example, of which (as in our other quotations from the 'Lieder ohne Worte') we give only the melody, is somewhat different.

MENDELSSOHN. 'Lieder ohne Worte, Book 2, No. 2.

Here the added bar (6a) is a free sequential repetition of the preceding bar, so far as the melody is concerned; the harmony again clearly shows it to be an accented bar.

244. Exceptionally it is possible to repeat the added bar itself sequentially, thus still further extending the length of the phrase. A very interesting example of this is shown in the following passage by Beethoven.

BEETHOVEN. Sonata in A, Op. 2, No. 2.

If the student will examine the movement from which we have taken the above, he will see at once that this is an after-phrase, beginning, as marked, with the fifth bar.   At bar 6 is an inverted cadence with feminine ending; this cadence is twice sequentially repeated in bars (6a) and (6b); and the bar (6c) is a further and

freer imitation of the preceding.   The whole after-phrase is thus
extended from four to seven bars.   We shall see presently that a
seven-bar phrase, or sentence, is usually a contraction from one of
eight bars.   Here it is evidently an extension ; but such a case as
this is exceptional.

245. As with unaccented bars (§ 240), we sometimes find
accented bars interpolated in both the fore- and after-phrase of a
sentence, producing a regular five-bar rhythm.

SCHUBERT.   Quartett in A minor, Op. 29.

Here the second bar, which we know to be an accented bar, is
repeated ; and the sixth bar is also repeated, though with some
variation both of melody and harmony.

246. In the last example to be given here of the interpolation
of an accented bar,

E. PROUT.   Piano Quartett, Op. 18.

the fore-phrase begins with a full cadence, the effect of finality
being prevented by placing the fifth of the tonic chord at the top.
The cadence is repeated in the following bar.   The after-phrase
corresponds exactly in construction to the fore-phrase.   It will be

seen that both here and in the passage by Schubert quoted in the last section, we get a perfectly satisfactory and complete sentence if we omit the repeated bars; but the effect of the passage would be entirely destroyed in both cases.

247. If the student will compare the two sentences last given with that seen in § 240, which is also in five-bar rhythm, he will find that the effect produced by the interpolation of an unaccented bar is quite different from that made by the addition of an accented bar. In the former case the cadence is deferred; in the latter, the result is to accentuate or emphasize the cadential feeling: although naturally this will not be so strong in the middle of a phrase as when the accented bar is added at the end, as in the examples given in the earlier part of this chapter.

248. We now come to speak of those cases in which the normal rhythm of four or eight bars is altered by contraction. Here we have the converse process to that of which we have been treating. The most common way in which this is effected is by the elision of an unaccented bar. Sometimes this will be the first bar of a phrase or sentence, as in the commencement of Mozart's overture to 'Figaro.'

MOZART.   'Figaro.'

In order to find out in such cases as this where the elision takes place, we must first ascertain by means of the cadences which are the accented bars, remembering that the principal cadences fall in the fourth and eighth bars. Here, although the passage is in unison, it will be seen at once that a half cadence is implied in the third, and a full cadence in the seventh bar. In fact, on the subsequent repetition of the passage with harmony above it, these cadences are found at the places we have indicated. These bars therefore mark the ends of the fore- and after-phrase; we accordingly mark them (4) and (8). By counting back from the cadences, we find that the first bar (an unaccented bar) is missing, and has been elided.

249. We have already learned that every regularly formed musical sentence consists of an alternation of accented and unaccented bars (§ 38), each unaccented bar being followed by an accented, exactly as in the motive the unaccented *notes* are followed by the accented. We also saw, in § 60, that it was very common for a sentence to begin with an incomplete motive, of which the unaccented part had been elided. The elision of the

unaccented bar at the beginning of a sentence, of which we are now speaking, is an exactly parallel case ; and the one does not really disturb the rhythm more than the other.

250. One of the most common examples of the elision of the unaccented bar at the beginning of a phrase is seen in the form of the Anglican chant—

FARRANT.

After what has been said in the last section, this chant requires no further explanation.

251. It is possible also to elide other bars than the first. One of the intermediate unaccented bars of a sentence may be elided, thus bringing two accented bars next to one another.

MENDELSSOHN. 'Lieder ohne Worte,' Book 5, No. 6.

Here is a sentence of sixteen bars, composed of two phrases of eight bars each. The fifth bar of the second phrase is elided. That it is an unaccented bar which is omitted is proved by the harmony of the passage.

252. In the following passage—

Bar 9.   MENDELSSOHN. 'Lieder ohne Worte, Book 3, No. 1.

we see the elision of the seventh bar, as well as an example of the extension of a sentence by (8 = 4), as in the passage quoted in § 234.

253. The student will observe that two accented bars can be brought next to one another in two ways,—either (as in our last two examples) by the elision of an unaccented bar, or (as in the examples given in §§ 242–246) by the interpolation of an accented bar. He must be careful to distinguish between these two methods ; and he never need be in any doubt as to which has been adopted, if he notices the total length of the phrase. The effect of elision is to reduce a four-bar to a three-bar phrase ; the effect of interpolation is to lengthen it to a five-bar phrase.

254. We spoke just now (§ 250) of the elision of the unaccented bar at the beginning of a phrase. Not infrequently both phrases of a sentence have the first bar elided ; in this case we have three-bar rhythm, just as in §§ 240, 245, 246, we saw five-bar rhythm.

HAYDN.   Quartett, Op. 20, No. 1.

255. This kind of rhythm is to be met with in some national airs. The old Scotch song " Leezie Lindsay " is a good example.

(a)   Old Scotch.

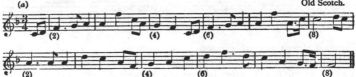

Another interesting specimen of the same rhythm is seen in the following Hungarian national air—

(b)   Hungarian Air.

The peculiar syncopated effects noticeable in this last melody are characteristic of Hungarian music.

256. It will be felt that the effect of the three-bar rhythm in the different passages last quoted is entirely satisfactory, in spite

of there being an uneven number of bars. After what has been
said in the earlier part of this volume as to the necessity of
balance, it would seem at first sight as if this ought not to be the
case.   That it is so nevertheless, is due to the fact that these
three-bar phrases each contain *an even number of accented bars.*
The passage from the overture to 'Figaro,' quoted in § 248,
sounds perfectly correct, though the first phrase contains three
bars, and the second four.   In the case of melodies, such as
those given in the last section, in which every phrase contains
three bars, the symmetry will be more readily perceptible; but
the following passage will prove that it is not indispensable that
elision should take place in all the phrases.

E. PROUT.   Concertante Duet, Op. 6.

This melody consists of four phrases, of which the first, second,
and fourth are three-bar phrases, while the third is of the normal
length of four bars.   In spite of this irregularity, which *a priori*
would seem as if it ought to disturb the balance, it will be felt
that the effect is perfectly satisfactory, and this can only be
accounted for by the fact that each phrase still contains the
regular number (two) of accented bars.

257. The well-known passage in the scherzo of Beethoven's
ninth symphony, where the composer has indicated '*Ritmo di tre
battute*' is often quoted as an example of three-bar rhythm. This,
however, is not a three-bar rhythm at all in the sense in which we
are now using the term.   It will be remembered that the scherzo

is in very rapid *tempo*, with only one beat in the bar, and that
therefore (like the passage from the quartett in E flat, given in
§ 71) the motives consist of two bars, and the movement is in
reality in $\frac{6}{4}$ time (compare the scherzo of the sonata, Op. 28,
quoted in § 40). The first theme of the scherzo now under
notice, if put into $\frac{6}{4}$ time, so as to show the position of the
accented bars, will appear as follows—

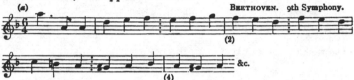

In the second part of this scherzo, the '*Ritmo di tre battute*'
(literally, 'Rhythm of three *beats*') shows, as there is only one
beat in a bar, that not every second, but every *third* bar is to be
accented; consequently this part of the movement is really in $\frac{9}{4}$
time.

In both this and the preceding example we have marked the
unaccented bars by dotted lines. It will be seen that there can
be no question here of the elision of an unaccented bar; it is
merely a change in the distance between the accented bars,
corresponding in what we may term the "larger metre" to a
change from duple to triple time.

258. We have seen earlier in this chapter that a sentence can
be extended by the interpolation of either an unaccented or an
accented bar. We cannot, however, contract a sentence or phrase
by the elision of an accented bar in the same manner as of an
unaccented. The nearest approach to this is the overlapping of
two phrases or sentences, produced by the conversion of the final
(accented) bar of one phrase into the first (unaccented) bar of the
following. This is not uncommon.

259. Our first example of this—

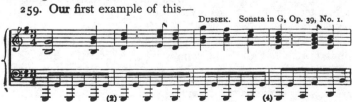

shows at the commencement a regularly constructed eight-bar sentence containing two phrases of four bars each.   On the last note of this sentence, the following one begins ; for the cadence in the last bar of our extract proves this to be the end of the fore-phrase, and therefore the fourth bar.   Counting back from this point, we see from the nature of the passage that the new sentence cannot possibly begin at (2) with the elision of an unaccented bar ; for this bar is too obviously a continuation of the preceding to allow of such an explanation.   Here therefore the eighth bar of the first sentence is also the first bar of the next, and we mark it accordingly (8 = 1).

260. In our next example the overlapping is, if possible, even clearer.

SCHUMANN.   2nd Symphony.

Here the second sentence begins at the eighth bar with the same subject as the first, though in a slightly modified form, and in the key of the relative major. At the eighth bar of this second sentence a full close is avoided, and the last four bars are repeated. We have therefore not marked the second (8) as (8 = 4) ; but, as the added phrase is merely a repetition of the last one, we mark its accented bars as (6a) and (8a). We have here an example of the repetition of the whole after-phrase.

261. A more familiar instance of this overlapping of two phrases is found in the following passage from the 'Lieder ohne Worte.'

MENDELSSOHN.   Lieder ohne Worte,' Book 3, No. 2.

262. If one of the unaccented bars of an eight-bar sentence or phrase be elided, *seven-bar rhythm* is produced. This, though less commonly met with than three-bar or five-bar rhythm, can hardly be described as rare. A very interesting specimen is found in the scherzo of Beethoven's great sonata in B flat, Op. 106.

BEETHOVEN.   Sonata, Op. 106,

This passage begins with a sentence of fourteen bars, made of
two seven-bar phrases. An examination of the harmony of the
passage shows us that in each phrase there is an elision of the
penultimate bar. It cannot be too strongly impressed on the
student, that the only way to determine with accuracy the form of
sentences of irregular construction is to examine the harmony of
the passage. In the first phrase here it is evident that down to
bar 6 there is a regular response to one bar by the next; as the
cadence occurs in the following bar, one bar sooner than expected,

it must be the seventh bar that has been elided.   After the
repetition of this phrase in the higher octave, ending with a full
close in the key of the dominant, we see a complete eight-bar
phrase without any elision, ending with a half cadence in C minor
(feminine ending).

263. Of the bar's rest which follows this phrase we will speak
directly; but first we will examine the after-phrase which completes this second sentence.   Like the two phrases of the last
sentence, it contains seven bars; but it is now the first bar of the
phrase (not, as before, the seventh) which is elided.   This is
most clearly proved by the harmony; for we find the dominant
harmony of C minor in the third and fifth bars, followed in the
fourth and sixth by the tonic harmony of the same key.   The
latter are therefore the accented bars, and the elision takes place
at the beginning of the phrase.   The bar's rest following the fore-
phrase is equivalent in its mental effect to a pause on the last
note of the phrase; for the mind always carries on the preceding
harmony through a rest.   Notice in this last phrase the change of
harmony on the unaccented beat by means of syncopation (§ 209).
The four phrases of this passage, which consists of 7 + 7 + 8 + 7
bars are in their seeming irregularity somewhat parallel to the
3 + 3 + 4 + 3 bars seen in § 256.

264. Another very good example of seven-bar rhythm is the
following—

MOZART.   Quartett in F, No. 23.

Here are two eight-bar sentences, each shortened to seven by the elision of an unaccented bar. In the first sentence the elision is that of the first bar of the after-phrase, and in the second sentence of the first bar of the fore-phrase, as the student, if he understands our principles of analysis, will at once see. The fore-phrase has 4 + 3 bars, the after-phrase 3 + 4.

265. It is not uncommon, especially at the beginning of a piece, to find one or two bars merely establishing a rhythmical figure, or a form of accompaniment to a principal melody, such bars not forming any part of the first sentence.

Here it is quite clear that the sentence begins in the second bar, and that the first bar merely indicates the rhythmic figure of the accompaniment. Several similar examples are to be found in Mendelssohn's 'Lieder ohne Worte,' and in many songs.

266. Not to be confounded with the case just mentioned is another frequently to be met with. We often find a piece beginning with an incomplete sentence, or (it would perhaps be more accurate to say) beginning in the middle of a sentence; for in such cases it will be always the first part of the sentence, not the last, which will be missing. Sometimes the first sentence will be simply preceded by the tonic—evidently to be taken as (8), the last note of a sentence.

Here a regular eight-bar sentence begins after the first note. We reckon this note as the last bar of a preceding sentence, of which all the rest is wanting, because, as we shall show immediately, we often meet with more than the final bar of a sentence used to commence a piece.

267. Haydn in several of his quartetts begins with a full cadence before commencing his principal theme. We give two examples.

HAYDN. Quartett, Op. 33, No. 5.

HAYDN. Quartett, Op. 71, No. 1.

In both these passages the opening bars are evidently the seventh and eighth of a sentence, that is to say the second (or *accented*) half of the after-phrase. We have already met with examples of the elision of an unaccented bar; here we have the elision of an unaccented section.

268. In our next extract we see the elision of an entire unaccented phrase (§ 50).

If it be asked Why are not the first four bars of this passage to be regarded as the fore-phrase, and the next four as the after-phrase? the answer is to be found in what follows, which we have not space to quote in full. For the sake of those students who do not know the sonata, we give the melody only of the continuation of the passage down to the end of the sentence. We start from the last bar of our previous quotation.

It will now be seen that, starting after the bar marked (8) in our example (*a*), we have a perfectly symmetrical sentence of sixteen bars, dividing into four four-bar phrases, and of the pattern $A + B + A + C$ with which we became acquainted in the last chapter (§ 190). It is quite clear that the opening four bars form no part of this sentence; they are an introductory after-phrase of which the fore-phrase is non-existent,—in other words, an abrupt commencement in the middle of a sentence.

269. In polyphonic compositions, such as fugues, the rhythms often become extremely complex, owing to the overlapping of phrases caused by fresh entries of the subject, sometimes at irregular distances.   Hence we very frequently find in such pieces interpolations and elisions of bars.   In some cases, however, a little thought will enable us to unravel the tangled web of parts, though passages are to be found in which it is necessary to "make believe a great deal" in order to trace the four-bar construction at all.

270.   To illustrate what has just been said, we will take an entire fugue from Bach's 'Forty-Eight,' and analyze it, with the needful explanations.

J. S. BACH   Wohltemperirtes Clavier, Fugue 36.

We have selected this fugue because its construction is comparatively simple. We shall nevertheless find in it irregularities of rhythm that we have not met with in the passages we have previously analyzed. With its form as a *fugue* we have here nothing to do ; that subject has been treated in an earlier volume of this series ; we are now concerned solely with its *rhythmical* structure.

271. The subject ends on the first note of the fourth bar, and being therefore of the length of the normal phrase, it renders the analysis much simpler. The answer follows immediately, and the first sentence ends in C minor at the eighth bar. A *codetta* (see *Fugue*, § 188) of three bars follows ; at the end of the third bar

the third voice enters with the subject. The cadence in F minor
at (a) shows the end of a phrase—therefore a fourth bar; but the
entry of the subject at the end of the preceding bar converts this
accented bar into the unaccented bar of the subject. Here
therefore we have the overlapping of two phrases (§ 258), and the
$(4 = 5)$ here indicated is similar to the $(8 = 1)$ seen in the examples,
§§ 259–261. The subject in the bass ends at bar (8); but it will
be seen that the cadence is prolonged by repetition in a varied
form at (b) (§ 228); we therefore mark the second cadence as (8a),
and the sentence is extended from eight to ten bars.

272. Let us now look ahead a little, to find out where the
next sentence ends. We see eight bars further on, at (c) an
inverted cadence in the key of E flat. This decidedly looks like
the end of a sentence; and our impression is strengthened by
finding at bar (4) an inverted cadence in A flat, or rather the
cadential harmony of dominant–tonic, for the G in the alto
prevents our regarding it as an ordinary inverted cadence. But
the sequential nature of the passage shows clearly the alternation
of accented and unaccented bars. Counting back from the
cadence at (c) we find that the eight-bar sentence begins at (b),
therefore we have here an example of overlapping, and the bar at
(b) is $(8a = 1)$.

273. The next two eight-bar sentences are quite regular,
except that at (d) the first of them ends with an interrupted
cadence, modulating into the key of the relative minor. It will
be seen that the fore-phrase of this sentence contains the subject
of the fugue, and the after-phrase the answer. The following
sentence, beginning at (d), contains the second episode.

274. The next entry of the subject in the bass (like the first
entry of the same voice) has its cadence prolonged at (e) by a
transposed repetition of the last two bars (4a); the sentence
$(4 + 2 + 4$ bars) ends on the dominant, and is immediately followed by another entry of the subject in the middle voice. The
first half of this sentence is quite regular; but at (f) we see the
interpolation of an unaccented bar (7a), for it is perfectly evident
that the sentence ends on the B flat in the bass. We find in
what immediately succeeds, the greatest rhythmic irregularity of
the whole fugue; it is only by careful examination that we can see
how to mark the following bars.

275. Looking ahead again from this point, we see that the bar
marked (g) and those which follow are precisely analogous to the
bars (6) (7) (7a) and (8) of our last sentence. The minim F in
the bass clearly shows the end of the sentence. This bar is
preceded, as before by two unaccented bars, and (g) is certainly
an accented bar, therefore (6). Counting back from this point,
we find two bars before (6) an inverted cadence (feminine ending)
in F minor, indicating another accented bar (4). We see therefore that this new sentence is incomplete, beginning with its

third bar (8 = 3), and that the whole first section of the fore-phrase has been elided.

276. After the explanations already given, the analysis of the rest of the fugue offers little difficulty.   At (*h*) we find an unac-cented bar (5a) interpolated, while the entry of the subject at the end of this bar causes another overlapping (6 = 1) in the next bar. The entry of the alto in stretto at (*i*) causes another contraction (4 = 5), while the (8 = 1) at the beginning of the coda at (*k*) is similar to that which we have already seen at (*b*).

277. We have intentionally selected one of the clearest of all Bach's fugues as regards its rhythmical structure; but it will be seen that out of eleven sentences that it contains not half are regular in form.   In the majority of fugues the elisions and extensions are far more frequent than in this one; indeed, so much is this the case, that one often entirely loses the feeling of the normal rhythm.   The student can easily convince himself of this by trying to analyze for himself such fugues as that in C major, in the first book of the 'Forty-Eight,' or those in D major and E major in the second.   The truth is, that a great many fugues cannot be stretched on the Procrustean bed of four- and eight-bar rhythm without doing great violence to their structure.   In such cases regularity of rhythm becomes an altogether subordinate matter; its place is supplied by regularity of accent.

278. A moment's thought will show us why this should be the case.   We know that by rhythm is meant "the more or less regular recurrence of cadences" (§ 9).   We also know that cadences are points of repose, dividing sentences and phrases (sometimes sections also) from one another.   But the peculiarity of fugue, and that in which it differs from nearly all other forms of composition, is its *continuity*.   Properly speaking, it has no points of repose; for though cadential formulæ are frequently employed, the last note of a cadence is always the point for a new departure.   Hence, as, in consequence of the continuity of the music, just spoken of, the want of repose is not felt, so neither can any ill effect be produced by the absence of regularity in the position of the cadences.   The ear accepts bar-accent as a sub-stitute for cadence.

279. We shall now analyze some passages from the works of the great masters, illustrating the various principles that have been laid down in this chapter.   Our first example is the commence-ment of one of Haydn's quartetts.

Allegro moderato.   HAYDN. Quartett, Op. 77, No. 1.

(4)   (6)

(8=4)   (4a)   (6)   (8)

This passage offers no difficulties in analysis, and is given as a fair average example of the kind of rhythmic irregularities frequently to be met with in the larger instrumental forms.   Our first business is to find out which are the accented bars.   The student should hardly need to be again reminded that they are those containing the cadences, or in which there is a change of harmony.   We see that the change to dominant harmony takes place here at the fifth bar.   This will consequently be (4); two bars earlier is another change of harmony, indicating (2); the sentence begins in the preceding bar, and we see that the first bar is the (8), the starting point, as in § 266.

280. The sentence is regularly constructed till its eighth bar; but as an inverted cadence is here substituted for a full cadence, we see that the end of the sentence has not been reached; another phrase is to follow.   We therefore mark this bar (8 = 4). The cadence is repeated (4a) in E minor in the following bar; and after this the sentence proceeds to its regular close at the eighth bar.   It will be seen that by the additions of a four-bar phrase (8 = 4) and a single bar (4a) the length of the sentence is extended from eight to thirteen bars without disturbing the feeling of symmetry.

281. The following passage shows much greater irregularity :—

Andante con moto.   SCHUBERT. Symphony in C, No. 7.

(2)   (4)   (6=4)

J

Here the cadence in the third bar clearly indicates a three-bar rhythm in the first phrase. But on examining the harmony closely, we find that we have **not** here the same kind of three-bar rhythm as in our examples, §§ 254, 255, in which the first unaccented bar was elided; for the incomplete dominant chord at the end of the first bar, followed by the tonic chord at the beginning of the second, gives the latter the feeling of an accented bar. It is the *third* bar of the phrase which is here elided, as in the example from Mendelssohn in § 252.   The after-phrase of the sentence we are now examining is considerably extended ; for we find no full cadence for seven bars.   The inverted cadence at (6) must therefore be regarded as the starting-point of a new phrase $(6 = 4)$.   Immediately afterwards we see the insertion of an unaccented bar (5a).   The sentence evidently ends at (8) ; but as the subject reenters on this note, we mark the bar $(8 = 1)$, as in the similar case in § 260.   As before, the third bar of this phrase is elided ; and an additional accented bar is introduced at (6a).

282. This second sentence is succeeded by another sentence containing two phrases of three bars each.   In these it is quite impossible to decide with certainty whether we should consider the first or the third bar to be elided, because every bar contains the same harmony.   We have therefore considered the first bar of each phrase as the one elided, because this is by far the most usual in three-bar rhythm.   Accordingly we mark the end of the second sentence $(8 = 2)$, though we might have also marked it $(8 = 1)$, as at the end of the first sentence.   Similarly, in the after-phrase, we regard the elision as that of the fifth, and not of the seventh bar. The last four bars of our extract show the resumption of the normal four-bar rhythm.

283. Our next example is one of the most interesting and instructive specimens of three-bar rhythm to be anywhere found.

Mozart.   Symphony in G minor.

Here the harmony leaves no doubt whatever as to its being the first bar of the phrase which is elided. The first sentence consists of eight bars reduced to six by the elision of bars 1 and 5. The second sentence, which begins at (*a*) contains exactly eight bars; it would nevertheless be a mistake to try to divide it into two four-bar phrases; for the harmony of the second bar is not cadential, while that of the third bar is so, proving that the third bar bears the stronger accent of the two. Besides this, the construction of the melody is almost identical with that of the two preceding phrases. It is clear that we have here again three-bar rhythm, with elision of the first bar; the phrase ends on (4), and the two bars (4a) and (4b) are repetitions of the cadence, such as we have already so frequently seen. An after-phrase of three bars, with elision of (5), completes the sentence.

284. The second part of the movement begins with three more three-bar phrases, the first two completing a sentence. At (*b*) is an inverted cadence which, with variations of form, is four times repeated in the following bars (4a–d). Observe that here these cadential repetitions, extending over four bars, do duty instead of the after-phrase of the sentence, which is never completed by a full cadence. At (*c*) the first subject returns, evidently beginning a new sentence (6 = 2). One bar later is a second entry of the subject (like a stretto of a fugue). In such cases, where two entries overlap, we reckon our rhythm *from the voice that last entered.* Here the third bar of the upper part is the second bar of the lower, and we mark the bar (3 = 2). At (4a) is seen the interpolation of an accented bar, after which the rhythm is regular to the end of the sentence, and two more three-bar phrases, similar to those at the beginning, complete the movement.

285. Our last example is one of Haydn's charming minuets— a form in which the composer was especially fond of sporting with varied and irregular rhythms.

HAYDN.   Quartett, Op. 76, No. 3.

After the full analyses we have given of the preceding examples, but few notes will be necessary here. The student will be sufficiently accustomed to our method of marking the bars to find little difficulty in following the structure of the music. It will be seen that the first sentence begins with an additional unaccented bar, as in the passage by Mozart, quoted in § 232. At (*a*) we find, as in our last example, cadential repetitions substituted for the after-phrase of a sentence. No further explanation ought to be required.

286. Before proceeding to speak of some other points that have still to be noticed in connection with irregular rhythms, we

must take this opportunity of disclaiming any attempt to dogma-
tize on this subject.　From whatever point of view it may be
looked at, it presents many difficulties to the theorist ; and we are
far from venturing to assert that the views propounded in this
chapter are the only correct ones.　It may even be possible that a
more satisfactory explanation may be found ; though we confess
that we have not been able to meet with one.　But the fundamental principle on which all the explanations in this chapter have
been founded—that all irregular rhythms are modifications of the
normal four-bar and eight-bar rhythm, either by extension or
contraction—has at least the advantages of being intelligible,
consistent, and (as may be seen from the large number of widely
differing examples analyzed by its means) capable of very large
and general application.　It is impossible to give the student any
rules as to when he should depart from the regular rhythmic form ;
but it may be said that such deviations are more admissible, and
mostly produce a better effect in larger than in smaller compositions.　But his own musical feeling (if he possess any) will be his
best guide in this matter ; and if, in addition to this, he carefully
studies, and endeavours to imitate, the practice of the great
masters, he is hardly likely to go very far astray.

287. A variety of rhythmic irregularity often to be met with,
and differing in some respects from those hitherto spoken of, is
that produced by *cross accents*, that is by making the accents come
otherwise than on the accented beats of the bar.　The simplest
and commonest case of this is syncopation, an example of which
will be found at § 209 (*b*).　A more complex disturbance of rhythm
is produced by grouping the notes of triple time in such a way as
to produce an impression of duple time, or the reverse.　The
former is much the more common of the two, and only a few
examples need be given.

Here the first phrase evidently begins with elision of an unaccented bar ; for the change from (implied) dominant harmony to

tonic at the third bar clearly shows the cadence ending the phrase; and the next bar (the real fourth from the beginning) is only a continuation of the same harmony, and cannot therefore be the accented bar. Here the grouping of the notes of the melody suggests $\frac{2}{4}$ time, and a charming effect is produced by the crossing of the bar-accent and the phrasing accent. The same effect is seen again in our next example.

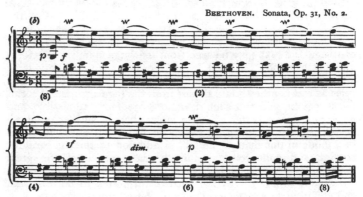

288. The close of the middle movement of one of Beethoven's piano and violin sonatas is a very beautiful example of the same effect in slow time.

289. In all the passages quoted above, the feeling of the triple time is maintained in spite of the cross accents. Sometimes, however, by means of dynamic indications the composer intentionally destroys for a while the feeling of the original time. It is impossible to play the following passage as Weber has marked it

without losing the feeling of triple time, and substituting for it
that of duple.

WEBER. Sonata in C, Op. 24.

It will usually be found in such cases of cross accent as these,
that the total numbers of bars in the phrase or sentence will be
normal, so that the balance of the whole is not disturbed. This
is the case, not only in the passage just quoted, but in both of
those given in § 287. In the example in § 288, we see only the
end of a sentence, with repetitions and prolongation of the final
cadence.

290. The converse process—grouping or accenting passages
in duple or quadruple time as if they were in triple—is much
rarer. The following passage, from the finale of Weber's 'Concertstück,'

WEBER. Concertstück.

looks at first sight as if it were an illustration ; but it will be seen
that though each bar contains three groups, and three accents
instead of two, yet, as these three only occupy the same time as

the regular two groups, the effect is rather analogous to the introduction of triplets in common time, *e.g.*, instead of

we have

291. The following curious passage from one of Schumann's
songs for children is much more to the point—

SCHUMANN. 'Von Schlaraffenland,' Op. 79, No. 5.

Here the first six bars are in reality four bars of $\frac{3}{4}$ time, and might
be written

As this is the beginning of the song, there can be no feeling of
cross accent here, because the regular accent of $\frac{2}{4}$ time has never
been established.   The position of the cadences in the second
and fifth bars would also be wrong were the time here really duple.

292. A better example of groupings of $\frac{3}{4}$ in common time is
seen in the following passage—

CLEMENTI.   Sonata, Op. 36, No. 3.

Here we never altogether lose the feeling of quadruple time, but the figures both of the upper and lower part are decidedly suggestive of $\frac{3}{4}$. The bass of this passage seems to have given Beethoven an idea for the well-known progression in unison in the first movement of his symphony in B flat. The following is another good example, in which a figure of six quavers is sequentially repeated in a passage of quadruple time—

BEETHOVEN. Sonata in F, Op. 5, No. 1.

293. Another variety of cross accent is that by which two bars of triple time are made to produce the effect of augmentation, that is to sound like one bar of double the length;—*e.g.*, two bars of $\frac{3}{8}$ like one of $\frac{3}{4}$, or two bars of $\frac{3}{4}$ like one of $\frac{3}{2}$. This effect is as old as Handel, as will appear from the following passage—

HANDEL. 'Rodrigo.

That Handel really felt this as $\frac{3}{4}$ time, is shown by the fact that he wrote it in that way when he subsequently introduced the melody in a slightly modified form into his oratorio 'Susanna.'

HANDEL. 'Susanna.'

A more familiar example of a similar procedure will be seen in the second subject of tbe finale of Schumann's piano concerto in A minor.

294. We have spoken above of the insertion and elision of one bar in a phrase. The insertion or elision of one beat in a bar is also possible, though very much rarer. No general principles can be given for this procedure, which can very seldom be adopted with good effect, and must, indeed, be regarded as altogether exceptional. A few examples are all that will be necessary here.

295. Our first illustration is from the works of Handel.

The third bar of the fore-phrase of this sentence is lengthened by the insertion of an accented beat, just as in several of the examples already given we have seen a sentence lengthened by the insertion of an accented bar.

296. The following passage

is an excellent example of the cross accents spoken of in § 287. The changes of harmony show us, as usual, the accented bars of the sentence. The sixth bar contains four crotchets instead of three, an accented beat being added, as in our last quotation.

297. The last example we give of an additional beat is of a different kind.

Here five crotchets, instead of four, are seen in the fourth bar of
our extract, thus delaying the return of the principal subject of
the movement in the following bar. In some editions the passage
has been corrected (?) by the omission of the first crotchet of the
third bar, and placing the following bar-line one crotchet later.
This, however, sacrifices the syncopated effect which was doubtless
intended by Mendelssohn at the beginning of this third bar. The
student will remember that a rest always carries on the mental
impression of the preceding harmony ; therefore a rest on an
accented beat, as here, produces the effect of the syncopation of
the preceding unaccented note. It would have been so easy for
Mendelssohn, had he wished, to have compressed the five crotchets
in the fourth bar into four—for example,

that we can hardly doubt that the additional crotchet here is
intentional.

298. It will be well to note here that the familiar passage in
the scherzo of Beethoven's 'Eroica' symphony in which triple
time is changed for four bars to duple—

BEETHOVEN. 3rd Symphony.

is not an example of the introduction of an additional beat in a bar, because *the length of the bar remains unchanged.* What is really altered is the *subdivision* of the bar, which is now divided into two parts, instead of into three. We have here, in fact, the converse case of that seen in our example in § 290.

299. The two following passages, showing the very rare elision of a beat in a bar, will need no explanation after what has been already said.

300. In concluding this chapter, a few words must be said concerning two other varieties of irregular rhythm—the so-called *quintuple* and *septuple* time, the former containing five beats in the

bar, and the latter seven.   Both of these are really irregular
compound times, the former being a combination of alternate bars
of triple and duple, and the latter of triple and quadruple time.
Both are rare, but quintuple time is much the less rare of the two.
Probably the earliest example of it is to be found in Handel's
opera ' Orlando.'   In the scene depicting the hero's madness,
which ends the second act of the opera, occurs the following
passage—

HANDEL. 'Orlando.

The grouping of the quavers here shows that Handel intended
the second accent of the bar to fall on the fourth quaver.   Here
therefore we have one bar of $\frac{3}{8}$ followed by one of $\frac{2}{8}$.

301. Sometimes when a movement is written in quintuple time
the places of the second accents are marked by dotted bars, as in
the following passage—

BOIELDIEU.   La Dame Blanche.'

Here a peculiar quaintness of effect is obtained by the alternations of triple and duple time. In the passage in $\frac{5}{4}$ time in the third act of 'Tristan und Isolde,' Wagner uses dotted bars in the same way.

302. The following passage, which is the opening of the slow movement of Chopin's sonata in C minor, is very curious.

Here there is much less regularity in the subdivision of the bars. In the first four bars it is difficult to say with certainty whether the second accent is intended to be placed on the third or fourth crotchet, though the *sforzandi* in the first two bars might seem to indicate the former. Again, in the fifth and seventh bars, the accent is clearly on the fourth crotchet, but in the sixth and eighth it seems rather to be on the third. Probably Chopin intended this ambiguous effect; but the result is hardly satisfactory.

303. As curiosities, and for the sake of completeness, we give as our last illustrations two specimens of the extremely rare septuple time. The first is found as an episode in the first movement of Liszt's 'Dante Symphony.'

Liszt. 'Dante Symphony.

Here we have alternate bars of $\frac{3}{4}$ and $\frac{4}{4}$ time, the subdivision of the larger bar being shown (as in the example from Boieldieu in § 301), by a dotted line.

304. Our second example is the very curious music representing the incantation of the Magi, in Berlioz's 'Childhood of Christ.'

Berlioz. 'L'Enfance du Christ.

K

Here $\frac{7}{4}$ is not marked as a time-signature; but in a note in the full score the composer says, "The beats in the triple time are of the same length as those of the quadruple, and the combination of the two bars must resemble a large bar with seven beats." The time is therefore really the same as in the passage by Liszt quoted above.

305. It will seldom, if ever, be advisable for the student to experiment with quintuple or septuple time, or even with the insertion or elision of a beat in a bar, though it was necessary here to explain such procedures. On the other hand, the extension and contraction of a sentence by the interpolation or elision of one or more bars may frequently be employed with advantage to prevent too great monotony, or 'squareness' of rhythm. Even this, however, should not be attempted till complete mastery has been obtained of the normal form treated of in the last chapter. Here, as in so many other cases, the general principle applies, that nobody can be trusted to break the rules until he thoroughly well knows how to keep them.

CHAPTER IX.

THE SIMPLE BINARY FORM.

306. In the preceding chapters of this volume we have explained in detail the construction of musical sentences, and have shown how they are built up on certain clear and easily recognizable principles from their component parts—viz. : phrases, sections and motives. We mentioned incidentally (§ 200) that it was rare to find a complete composition consisting of only one sentence. We have now to show how sentences are to be combined with one another to form larger wholes. The simplest musical form is that which contains two complete sentences, and which naturally divides itself into two parts. For this reason it is called the *Binary* or *Two-Part Form.*

307. One of the most interesting points to the student of composition, is the way in which the larger forms are developed, as by a kind of organic growth, from the smaller. We have already seen this with the sentence, which is sometimes made out of a single motive. We examined sentences of various forms (§§ 187–193), and we found that the phrases and sections into which they are divided were sometimes similar, and sometimes contrasted. In the short pieces which we are now going to examine, consisting of only two sentences, we shall find in the same way symmetry and contrast ; and the various formulæ which we gave in § 207 for the construction of a single sentence will apply also to pieces containing two sentences. We shall also see as we proceed that it is possible to extend or contract one or both of the sentences without necessarily disturbing the form of the piece, just as we found in the last chapter that the phrases and sections of the same sentence were capable of extension and contraction by the interpolation or elision of bars, or (more rarely) of single beats.

308. Among the simplest examples of binary form are hymn-tunes four lines in length, and double chants. As an example of the former may be given the well-known tune ' Dundee.'

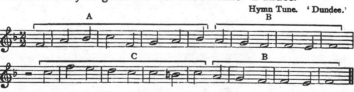

Hymn Tune. ' Dundee.'

The tune is so familiar that it is needless to give more than the melody. It will be seen that it consists of two sentences, both ending with a full cadence in the tonic key, and each containing two phrases. The fore-phrase of each sentence is different; but the after-phrase is identical. The form therefore is A + B + C + B, with which we are already acquainted.

309. Our next example is formed on the same plan, but the whole of the first sentence is repeated, and the after-phrases are extended by prolongation of the cadences from four to five bars.

Choral. "Liebster Jesu, wir sind hier."

310. The very concise binary form of which we are now speaking is comparatively rare, excepting in simple songs (such as national airs and Volkslieder), dances, and themes for variation. We occasionally find it, nevertheless, as an independent form. We give two short specimens by Schumann.

SCHUMANN. Papillons, No. 1.

Here are two eight-bar sentences, the former divided into two four-bar phrases, while the latter is undivided (compare § 187). A curious point about this piece is the very remote modulation to A flat at the beginning of the second sentence. It is extremely rare in such short pieces as this to find a modulation to an unrelated key.

311. Our next example is more regular in its course of modulation.

SCHUMANN.   'Bunte Blätter,' Op. 99, No. 1.

This little piece contains two eight-bar sentences, each divided into two phrases. The fore-phrase of the first sentence ends with a half cadence in the tonic key, while the after-phrase modulates to the dominant. In the second (responsive) sentence, the fore-phrase modulates to the supertonic minor (relative minor of the subdominant), and the after-phrase returns to the tonic.

312. Now let us look at the material from which the piece is constructed. We see that the first and second phrases begin with the same theme,

which is also found in a somewhat different form at the commencement of the fourth phrase. The latter half of each phrase is

varied, because each one leads up to a different cadence. The
third phrase consists of altogether new ·material. The formula
(§ 188) for the whole piece, counting the phrases as units, will
therefore be, A + A* + B + A*.

313. Many pieces of dance music are to be· found containing
only two short sentences, like the pieces just examined. Our first
specimen will be a Gavotte from one of Corelli's 'Sonate da
Camera à tre,' for stringed instruments.

This little piece is rather curious in more than one respect. In
the first place, each of the sentences contains only four bars,
instead of eight. We know that quadruple time is really compound time (§ 36), each bar containing two accents ; but a gavotte
usually consists of at least sixteen bars of quadruple time. Moreover, it ought to begin on the *third* beat of a bar, and not on the
first, as will be seen in an example that we shall give later (§ 323).
A further irregularity is found in the fact that all the cadences here
have feminine endings. These details, however, do not affect the
point we are now illustrating—the construction of short pieces by
putting together two sentences of equal length.

314. Mozart's charming Dances, many of which were written
for the royal balls at Vienna, consist, with few exceptions, of a
series of little pieces, each sixteen bars in ·length. Each piece is
followed by a second, called a 'Trio' precisely similar in form,
after which the first is repeated. We give one of the Minuets,
with its Trio, as an example.

(8) *Da Capo.*

Each of these pieces is by itself a complete specimen of the short binary form that we are now considering; while the two taken together constitute an example of ternary form, of which we shall speak in the next chapter.   If we examine the four phrases of which the minuet is composed, we see that the first and third are quite different, while the fourth is a transposition of the second from the key of the dominant to that of the tonic.   The formula is therefore $A + B + C + B^*$.   In the Trio, on the other hand the second and fourth phrases are variations of the first, the formula being $A + A^* + B + A^*$.

315. Of the large number of waltzes and other dances written by Schubert, the greater part (considerably over 200 pieces) are in the form under notice.   We give one of the waltzes, as our last example of dance music.

SCHUBERT.   'Trauer-Walzer, Op. 9, No. 2.

We have chosen this number because of its containing a modulation to a key (the flat submediant major) which is only in the
second degree of relationship.   It ought to be hardly necessary to
remind readers that the key of E major, to which the modulation
is here made, is really F flat.

316. In themes for variations the sixteen-bar double-sentence
form is often met with, as in the theme of Beethoven's variations
in G major, beginning

We give a less familiar but very beautiful example by Haydn.

HAYDN.   Symphony in C, No. 60.

317. It is by no means uncommon in this concise binary form
to find that the first eight bars end with a half-cadence.   In this
case, we consider the whole piece to contain two complete sentences, though it is really formed from one long sixteen-bar

sentence divided into four phrases.   It must be remembered that
the eight-bar period is our unit of measurement, and we therefore
regard it as a sentence in many cases where it ends with a half-
cadence (§ 47).   An example of this form is the contredanse in
Beethoven's 'Prometheus,' which he later used as the theme for
his Variations, Op. 35, and for the finale of the 'Eroica' symphony.

318. Another class of composition in which the small binary
form is often met with is the song.   Many of our most popular
national melodies are of this construction ; among them we may
mention such well-known airs as "The blue-bells of Scotland,"
"The last rose of summer," "By the banks of Allan water," and
"The Vicar of Bray."   Each of these melodies contains two
sentences, both ending with a full close in the tonic key, and with
incidental modulations to nearly related keys.   In other examples,
such as "Hearts of Oak" or "The Lass of Richmond Hill," the
first sentence ends with a modulation.

319. Though in vocal music the form of composition is often materially influenced by the words to be set, this is hardly at all the case in "strophic" songs—that is, songs in which every stanza (or "strophe") of the poem is sung to the same music. We give two examples of this form from the works of the great masters.

WEBER. ' Liebeslied,' Op. 54, No. 3.

We have chosen this little melody as one of the shortest examples we can find of a complete piece in regular binary form. Like the little song by Schumann given in § 200, it contains only eight bars; but whereas that example consisted of only one sentence, we have here two, each four bars in length, and divided into phrases of two bars—or, to speak more accurately, the first sentence divided into two phrases, and the second less clearly divided. This is a parallel case to that which we saw in the seventh chapter (§ 201) with respect to a single sentence. The $\frac{2}{4}$ time here is really $\frac{4}{8}$, containing two accents in the bar; each four-bar sentence therefore has the usual number of accents. The last two bars are the concluding symphony to the song, and furnish an example of the repeated and varied cadence.

320. The following song by Mozart

MOZART. Song, 'Im Frühlingsanfang.'

begins with the end of a sentence (see § 266), for it is clear that
the chord of E flat at the commencement forms no part of the
first phrase.   We have here two eight-bar sentences, the first
ending with a full cadence in the key of the dominant.   The
construction of the melody is quite symmetrical, the form being
the same as in the trio of the minuet given in § 314, viz. :
A + A* + B + A*.   As in our last example, we find a repetition
of the final cadence as a concluding symphony.

321. Hitherto we have been examining only those very small
and simple forms which consist of two eight-bar sentences ; and
we have said that such are somewhat rare.   When the binary form
assumes larger dimensions, we seldom find it divided by the
cadences with such regularity.   When in the last chapter we
introduced the subject of extension and contraction of sentences
(§ 221), we showed that the object of such processes was to avoid
the monotony resulting from too great uniformity.   It is not often
(at all events in modern music) that absolute uniformity of rhythm
is maintained for more than sixteen bars, excepting in dance
music.   In the last two examples we have quoted we have seen a
repetition of the final cadence introduced for the sake of variety.
The minuet now to be given from one of Haydn's quartetts shows
a different manner of avoiding monotony.

HAYDN.   Quartett, Op. 64, No. 4.

322. If the student will count the bars of this minuet, he will
see that there are 32, or exactly the length of four eight-bar
sentences. The first part is quite regular, containing a sentence of
two four-bar phrases, and closing in the tonic key. The second
part commences with a four-bar phrase, which is prolonged by
cadential repetitions, first of two bars each (4a and 4b) then of
one bar (4c). From this point begins the return to the tonic key;
and the responsive phrase of this second sentence ends, not with
a full cadence in D, but with a half cadence in G (compare the
the example in § 317, where the first sentence also ends with a

half cadence).   We therefore mark the close of this sentence
(8 = 4).   We know that the sentence ends where we have marked
it, because the concluding sentence is an exact repetition of the first
one.   As this second sentence ends on the dominant, we also know
that the corresponding bars preceding will be the accented bars.
This enables us to fix the position of (6) with its repetition (6a),
and also shows that we have the interpolation of an unaccented
bar (5a).   The middle part of the minuet, containing the modulation to the dominant, and the return to the original key, therefore
consists of one eight-bar sentence extended to sixteen bars.   The
formula for the whole minuet is A + B + A, in which the second
part, B, is exactly double the length of A ; the balance and proportion of the whole piece is therefore perfect.

323. Our next illustration is somewhat different in form.

J. S. BACH.   'Französische Ouverture.

(4)

(8)

Notice in the first place that here the cadences come regularly at
every fourth bar throughout the piece. This is because the
movement is a Gavotte—one of the old dance-forms; we have
already said that absolute uniformity in the position of the
cadences is more often to be found in dance music than in any
other kind of composition The time-signature here given by
Bach is equivalent to the more frequently used ₵, and shows that
there are two beats in a bar, the minim being the unit of measurement. The piece consists of three sentences, the first of which
modulates to the key of the relative major, the most frequent first
modulation, as we already know (§ 82), for a piece in a minor key.

324. The second sentence introduces a modulation in its fore-
phrase to A major, while the after-phrase ends in F sharp minor,
the dominant minor of the original key. The third and final
sentence returns through E minor to the original tonic, its fore-
phrase ending with a half cadence, and its after-phrase, of course,
with a full cadence in that key. It will be seen that, with the
exception of G major, modulations are made to all the nearly
related keys to B minor, but that in no case is more than one
cadence made in any other key than the tonic. In small forms,
such as those which we are now discussing, *modulation should
never be made twice to the same key.*

325. Before leaving this passage, let the student examine the
thematic material from which it is constructed. It will be seen
that the two motives of the first bars

are almost continuously employed throughout the movement: for
the semiquaver figure in the bass of the second bar is only the
diminution of the four quavers in the treble of the preceding bar.
A careful analysis will show that one or other of these two motives
is to be found in nearly every bar except in the final cadences to

the three sentences. The whole gavotte furnishes a practical
illustration of what was said in Chapter VII. as to the treatment
of the motive.

326. Our next illustration shows another variety of the same
form; it is the slow minuet which forms the third movement of
the overture to Handel's opera ' Berenice.'

HANDEL.   ' Berenice.

The first part of this piece contains two sentences of eight bars
each, instead of only one, as in our preceding examples; the

L

second sentence closes in the dominant key. The second part of
the movement begins with a return to the original key, from which
a modulation is made to the relative minor. After a full close in
that key the music returns to the original tonic, and a new idea is
presented in the short canon in the octave at one bar's distance.
The sentence is completed at the eighth bar, though there is only
a half cadence here (§ 317). It leads to the repetition of the
opening subject; and as this has not now to lead into the dominant key, it is furnished with a new continuation, its after-phrase
being repeated for a final close. The second part of the minuet
therefore, contains three sentences, the last of which is extended
by repetition of the after-phrase from eight bars to twelve.

327. The Bourrée (one of the older dance-forms) from Bach's
sixth 'Suite Française' is a good illustration of the use of irregular
rhythms in the small binary form.

Of the four sentences found in this little piece, only one is of the normal length of eight bars. The first and second are each extended to twelve bars by the addition of a third phrase; the third sentence is regular in length; and in the fourth there is an extension of two bars in the after-phrase. The double counterpoint in this very interesting little piece will repay careful examination.

328. We have already seen (in §§ 319, 320) the application of the very concise binary form of two eight-bar sentences in vocal music. The somewhat larger form which we are now considering is also frequently to be met with in vocal works. Most of the pieces known as 'Cavatinas' are in binary form. As familiar examples may be cited the song "Porgi amor" in Mozart's 'Figaro,' the two airs in Haydn's 'Seasons,' "Distressful nature fainting sinks," and "Light and life dejected languish," and, as a more modern instance, "Be thou faithful unto death" in Mendelssohn's 'St. Paul.' Handel also frequently employs this form, both in his operas and in his oratorios. We give a very beautiful and little known example—the air "Convey me to some peaceful shore," from the oratorio 'Alexander Balus.'

The construction of this piece is so simple that it requires but little explanation.   We have here a very good example of the commencement of a movement in the middle of a sentence (§§ 266–268).   An examination of the music shows clearly that a new sentence begins after the full cadence in the fifth bar—that is, with the entry of the voice.   Counting back from this point we find that the introductory symphony begins on a fourth bar, which we number accordingly.   There is a similar elision of the first half of a sentence in the concluding symphony.   The rest of the piece is quite regular in form.

329. In an earlier part of this volume it was said, in speaking of quadruple time (§ 36), that it was necessary in many cases, in order to ascertain the rhythm, to regard each bar as equivalent to two.   It will be seen that in our last example (as well as in some previously given) we have not done this.   In order to decide whether a bar of four crotchets in length is to be considered as one bar or two, it is always necessary to examine the harmonic structure of the music.   In Handel's song we see that, with one single exception, each bar contains only two chords.   Clearly the minim is here the unit of measurement; and it is probable that Handel, if he thought about the matter at all, only abstained from

marking the time-signature as ₵, because that might have given an erroneous impression as to the *tempo* of the music. We have here in reality only two beats in the bar, and the time is an extremely slow *alla breve.* In § 319 we have seen the converse case—$\frac{2}{4}$ treated as quadruple time. The rhythm will be in all cases determined by the position of the cadences.

330. The simple binary form sometimes assumes larger dimensions than in the examples hitherto given. We have already quoted passages in which the first part ended with a modulation to some nearly related key (§§ 323, 326, 327); not infrequently there will be a complete sentence (sometimes with extensions) in this secondary key, almost sufficient in importance to be termed a second subject. In such a case this secondary theme is often repeated in the tonic key in the second part of the movement. This form is seen, at least in its outline, in the examples by Bach in §§ 323 and 327, and it is to be found in many of the Preludes in the second part of the 'Wohltemperirtes Clavier.' As one of the clearest and most instructive specimens of it, we give the Prelude in G major.

J. S. BACH. Wohltemperirtes Clavier, Prelude 39.

(8=6)   (8)

331. The division of this prelude into its sentences and phrases required a little care; it will, however, be found quite intelligible by those who have grasped the principles laid down in the last chapter as to extension and contraction of sentences. The first sentence is contracted by the overlapping of its two phrases (§ 258), and the second sentence begins on the last note of the first one (8 = 1); the former therefore does not end with a full cadence. The after-phrase of this second sentence is extended by two bars, by means of an interrupted cadence, which changes the eighth to a sixth bar. The whole of this last sentence, from its second bar is in the key of the dominant.

332. The second part of the movement commences with a modified form of the opening theme, now leading back from D, through the tonic key, to C, the subdominant, in which key the sentence ends. As before, the two phrases of this sentence overlap. The following sentence shows an elision of its first two-bar section. It is quite clear that the full cadence in E minor marks the end of a sentence where we have marked it at (8); counting back from this point, we find the close of the fore-phrase at (4) no less distinctly indicated by the half cadence in the same key. Just as we saw in § 268 an entire fore-phrase elided, we have here the first (unaccented) *section* of the fore-phrase elided. The following sentence is quite regular in structure; it ends with a half, instead of a full cadence, as we have frequently seen is the case in the intermediate sentences. In the last sentence of this Prelude both phrases are extended to six bars; in the fore-phrase the extension is made by the sequential repetition of the first section; while the after-phrase, from (*b*) to the end, is a somewhat modified transposition into the key of the tonic of the subject which at (*a*) in the first part of the movement was given in the key of the dominant. This is the point that we particularly wish to illustrate in giving this prelude as one of our examples—the

repetition in the tonic of a theme which in the first part of the movement has been heard in some other key.

333. In other examples of this form, and especially in those of comparatively more modern composers, such as Haydn and Mozart, we find still greater symmetry between the two parts of the movement.   As a very interesting specimen we give the following Adagio by Mozart—

This movement deserves a somewhat detailed analysis of its construction, both from a rhythmical and thematic point of view. Its two-part form is very clearly marked by the fact of each half being repeated. The first part contains twenty-four bars, which, however, are not divided (as might perhaps have been expected) into three sentences of eight bars each. Instead of this, we find first a sentence of the normal length, and then a sentence extended by interpolations and repetitions of cadence from eight to sixteen bars. We have already met with a somewhat similar case in the minuet by Haydn given in § 321.

334. It will be seen that the materials of which the first and second sentences are constructed are not only different, but we might almost say contrasted. The first sentence is in F minor, its fore-phrase ending with an interrupted cadence, and its after-phrase with a full cadence in that key. The second sentence begins at once in A flat, the relative major key. In spite of its irregular length, its rhythmical analysis offers not the slightest difficulty, if we bear in mind our guiding rule that the bars in which the cadences are found are the accented bars, and that the most decided cadences indicate the fourth and eighth bars of a sentence. We see that the fore-phrase is of the regular length of four bars, and that the half cadence with which it concludes is repeated (4a) two bars later. At (5a) we see the interpolation of an unaccented bar (§ 238); it is quite clear that we should be

wrong to consider this bar as the sixth and the next one as the seventh, because the harmony shows the latter to be an accented bar as compared with the former.   Three bars later the interrupted cadence changes the eighth bar to a sixth, and the full cadence in A flat is the true eighth bar.   Two cadential repetitions (§ 227) conclude the first part of the piece.

335. The second part of this Adagio consists of three sentences, the first of which ends with a half cadence.   Excepting that the first bar is a modification of the opening motive of the movement, this sentence is formed entirely of new material.   The second sentence begins with the resumption of the first subject in the key of the dominant minor, modulating for the after phrase to the original tonic, F minor.   This phrase is extended by two bars, and is identical with the opening sentence of the first part, with the omission of two bars.   The concluding sentence (eight bars extended to eighteen) should be carefully compared with the second sentence of the first part.   It will be seen that what was there in A flat major is here repeated, with slight modifications, in F minor ; we have at (4a) the same extension of the fore-phrase by repetition of the half cadence ; we have the same interpolation of an unaccented bar at (5a); the only difference of any importance is, that the after-phrase is two bars longer than before—the interrupted cadence (8 = 6) occurring twice instead of once.   The entire movement may be analyzed thus :

First Part.

First sentence (F minor)—8 bars.
Second sentence (A flat)—16 bars.

Second Part.

Intermediate sentence—8 bars.
Modified repetition of first sentence (C minor and F minor)—10 bars.
Modified repetition of second sentence (F minor)—18 bars.

336. Of all the varieties of the binary form of which we have spoken, the one just noticed is the most important, because it is, as will be seen in the next volume of this series, the germ out of which the modern sonata form was·developed.   Those students who are already acquainted with this form will have no difficulty in tracing it here in embryo.   We have seen how this larger binary form is in its essentials an extension of the smaller forms explained in the earlier part of this chapter ; and we find here one more illustration of what we then described as the " organic growth " of the larger forms from the smaller.

337. The Binary form in the various shapes in which we have seen it is called by many writers the " two-part Song-Form," or " Lied-Form."   We have not employed this name in the present chapter because in many cases it would be quite inappropriate.

It is true that a large number of songs—we might probably say the larger number—are written in this form,—but it is used quite as often for instrumental as for vocal compositions. It seems little short of nonsense to talk of Bach's Prelude given in § 330 as being "in song-form," when it has not the least resemblance to a song. It would be quite as fitting to call the Binary the "two-part Dance-Form," considering that by far the larger number of dances are in binary form. The absurdity of such a name will appear at once if we think of applying it to such a piece as the song "He shall feed his flock" in the 'Messiah,' which unquestionably belongs to this category. Yet the one name is not more inappropriate than the other; and the best plan is to use the comprehensive generic term 'Binary,' as we have done throughout this chapter.

338. The student can now begin to write short pieces in binary form according to the various models given him in this chapter. To assist him, we shall conclude with a few general rules and principles which may guide him in cases of doubt, and guard him from some of the mistakes most frequently made by beginners. It will be well for him to commence with the very simplest and most regular forms before proceeding to the larger forms in which extended or contracted sentences are employed.

339. The easiest kind of composition with which to begin will be a hymn-tune of what is known as 'Long Metre,' which consists of two eight-bar sentences, each divided into two phrases by a middle cadence of some kind. In composing such a tune it will be advisable to make the first sentence end with a modulation to a nearly related key,—the best and most usual being to the dominant for a tune in a major, and to the relative major for a tune in a minor key. It is not very uncommon to find the first sentence, as well as the second, ending with a full close in the tonic key; but in such a short piece it is generally better not to introduce the same cadence twice. We have already warned the student (§ 324) against making the same modulation twice. There must also be variety in the middle cadences which end the fore-phrase of each sentence. The fore-phrase of the first sentence not infrequently ends with a full close in the tonic key, as in the examples to §§ 311, 317; but it would be very weak to use this cadence for the fore-phrase of the *second* sentence, because we should then have the same cadence twice in succession—at the end of the third and fourth lines of the tune. The middle cadences may be either half cadences, inverted cadences, or full cadences in some nearly related key to the tonic.

340. What is to lead up to these different cadences must be left to the student himself. We said in the first chapter of this volume that it was impossible to teach the invention of melody; and only the most general hints can be given as to the construction of the different phrases of which the tune will be composed

It will be well to remember that there should be some kind of connexion between the parts of the tune, though it is not easy to define in what the connexion should consist. Often the development of the melody from one or two motives will effect this; sometimes sequential passages may be introduced with advantage. But if the student have any aptitude for composition, his own musical feeling will be his best guide.

341. We now give a few outlines for hymn tunes, marking the number of bars, and indicating the basses of the cadences.

These outlines can be filled up in many different ways; and the student should write at least two or three tunes to each of them. He should be aware that if a melody begins with an incomplete bar the length of the last note will most probably give the completion of that bar (*Counterpoint*, § 513). In order, therefore, to determine the length of the first note of his tune, he must look at the last note, and deduct the value of that note from that of a whole bar.

342. Each of these tunes is provided with different cadences. To illustrate a very common form, we have made the first half of the second tune end with a half cadence in the tonic, instead of with a modulation to the dominant. It will also be seen that the

fourth tune is of a different metre to the others—that known as
'Eights and Sevens.'   Here each line begins with an accented,
instead of an unaccented note, and the first and third lines have
feminine endings.   We have also introduced one of the less
frequent modulations at the end of the first sentence.

343. Having written various tunes on the outlines given above,
the student should next write others, selecting his own cadences.
He need not now confine himself to the metres of which we have
given examples, but may experiment with other forms for himself.

344. The next step in composition should be the writing of
little pieces of sixteen bars in other forms than that of the hymn
tune.   A very useful exercise will be the *paraphrasing* of the
various examples given in this chapter—that is, the writing of
other pieces in exactly the same form, but constructed of different
materials.   As an example of what is meant, we give a paraphrase
of the minuet by Mozart in § 314.

If this piece (which is written merely as an exercise, and has no
pretension to other musical value) be compared with the original,

M

it will be seen that it follows its outline very closely. All the cadences are identical, the second bar of the second phrase is a repetition of the first, and the fourth phrase is the transposition of the second from the key of the dominant to that of the tonic. This example will sufficiently show the student how to write similar ones for himself.

345. After writing a number of such paraphrases as we have indicated, the student may attempt original pieces in the same form. He should then begin to compose little pieces with more than two sentences. If he writes a piece with three sentences, it will be better to let the first part contain one sentence, and the second two, as in the example to § 323, rather than the converse; for it must be remembered that the second part of the piece is the response to the first, and therefore should be the weightier, if there is any difference between the two. The third sentence may be either constructed of new material, or it may be a repetition of the first sentence, with or without variation. It must, of course, be varied if the first sentence ends otherwise than with a full close in the tonic key.

346. It will not be advisable, with this simple binary form, to let a piece exceed four sentences in length. If there are four sentences, there can either be two in each part, or one in the first and three in the second. In all these larger pieces care must be taken to obtain as much variety of cadence as possible; and in modulating, the student must be very careful as to the order of keys chosen. Remember especially that with a piece in a major key, it is almost always bad to make the first modulation to the key of the subdominant; for the subdominant is the key in which the original tonic is the dominant; and a modulation to this key soon weakens the feeling of the original tonality, if made too early. On the other hand, after making a modulation to the dominant side of the key, it is often best to let the next modulation be to the subdominant side; one modulation counterbalances the other, and the impression of the original key remains unimpaired.

347. It will be well, in conclusion, to give the student a few hints as to the use of the sentences of irregular length treated of in our last chapter. Our first advice will be, not to use them at all until he is thoroughly accustomed to writing sentences of the normal eight-bar form. He will then be able to extend his sentences by the addition of a third phrase: *i.e.*, by means of our familiar formula (8 = 4). He can also extend and repeat his cadences (§§ 227–231). He may next introduce the repetition, with or without variation, of a single section (§§ 233, 234). The interpolation of a single bar (§§ 238–247) will be found more difficult to effect satisfactorily, and here the student's musical feeling must come to his aid. It is worse than useless to introduce a bar merely for the sake of making the rhythm irregular.

Five-bar phrases are not very common, and should not be used unless for some particular effect which cannot be otherwise obtained. The same is true of the elision of a bar, producing three-bar phrases. It is always easy to tell whether such phrases of irregular length are employed with artistic intention, or whether they are the result of clumsiness or carelessness on the part of the composer. On the other hand, the contractions produced by the overlapping of two sentences $(8 = 1)$ may often be introduced with excellent effect, though (it should be added) more frequently in the larger forms to be treated of in our next volume than in the small form with which we are now dealing. On the whole, it is comparatively seldom that in pieces in simple binary form it will be expedient to introduce any other irregularity of rhythm than the addition of a third phrase to a sentence $(8 = 4)$, or the repetition of a final cadence (8a, 8b, &c.).

CHAPTER X.

THE SIMPLE TERNARY FORM.

348. We now come to the consideration of one of the most important, and perhaps the most frequently employed, of all musical forms,—that known as the *Ternary Form.* By the word "Ternary" is meant that which divides into three parts, just as by the "Binary" form, treated of in the last chapter, is designated a form which divides itself into two parts. This form is often called the 'Three-part Song Form,' just as the Binary Form is also known as the 'Two-Part Song Form.' For the reasons given in § 337, we do not adopt the alternative name.

349. It is an unfortunate thing that great difference exists among theorists as to the nomenclature of the different musical forms. For instance, the minuet by Haydn given in § 321 as an example of binary form would be considered by some authorities to be ternary; while some of the examples that we shall give in the course of this chapter are described in Marx's 'Composition' as Rondos. It is true that the various forms sometimes resemble one another so nearly, that a little careful examination is necessary to decide to which class a particular piece may belong; it is therefore all the more desirable that we should have some distinct line of demarcation whereby we may distinguish one form from another.

350. In order to illustrate this point, let us turn to the example (just referred to), in § 321, and show why we consider it as being in binary, and not in ternary form. Those who adopt the latter designation would say that the first eight bars form the first part of the movement, the following sixteen bars, the second, and the repetition of the first eight bars, the third part. The objection to this method of dividing the movement is, that the second part is not contrasted with the first, but is simply a continuation of it. A true ternary form should always contain an *episode* of some kind. By the word "episode" is meant a subject altogether distinct from the principal subject of the piece, and more or less strongly contrasted with it. It will be seen that this description will not apply to the middle portion of the minuet by Haydn of which we are now speaking.

351. If the student will now turn to the minuet and trio by Mozart, given in § 314, of which we remarked that while each piece separately regarded was in binary form, the two together,

with the repetition of the minuet, constituted a ternary form, he will at once see the difference between this example, and that by Haydn in § 321. Here the trio is clearly contrasted with the minuet ; we do not describe it as an episode, because it forms a distinct whole by itself ; but it possesses an episodical character, inasmuch as its subjects are altogether different from those of the minuet.

352. In a genuine ternary form, *the first part of the movement will always be in itself a complete binary form* ; that is to say, it will contain at least two sentences (§ 306), of which the second should end with a full cadence in the tonic key ; otherwise it is evident that the binary form will not be complete. The second part of the movement may also be a complete binary form—as in the case of the trio of a minuet ; but perhaps more frequently, instead of ending with a full cadence, the middle portion of the movement leads back to the return of the first part. We must add that, in the very large majority of cases, this middle part will be in a different key from the first. Occasionally in the case of a minuet and trio, the latter will be in the same key as the former, as in our example to § 314 ; but this is not very common. The third part of the movement will be a repetition of the first, either wholly or partially ; not infrequently the first part is considerably varied. A free *coda**—that is, a tail-piece or concluding portion, which may be, but is not necessarily, constructed from subjects previously heard, may be added at the discretion of the composer.

353. It is essential to the unity of the composition as a whole, that the third part of a ternary movement should contain the principal idea of the first part. Often we find it very considerably altered, sometimes only one sentence of the first part is repeated ; but the third part is never constructed, like the second, from new material.

354. The general outline of the form just given can be filled up in an almost infinite variety of ways ; and the examples which we are about to give will show that it is far more elastic than the binary form ; we find specimens of it, in fact, in almost every department of music.

355. Our first illustration will be one of the shortest and simplest examples of a complete ternary form that we can find. The three parts are indicated by Roman numerals (I., II., III.).

Andante.
(I.)	BEETHOVEN. Sonatina, Op. 79.

p espress

---

* Italian, *coda*=a tail.

Notice first the rhythmic construction of this piece, which, though hardly to be described as rare, is not very frequently met with. The time is compound, each bar containing three bars of $\frac{3}{8}$ time. Here is a case in which we distinctly have a second accent on the third beat of the bar.   Dr. Riemann, in his 'Catechism of Composition' explains this passage as being in $\frac{6}{8}$ time, with the elision of the unaccented beat of each alternate bar, thus—

Whether this ingenious explanation be adopted or not, there can be no doubt that each bar here contains two accents, and that each sentence is four bars in length, instead of eight.   It must never be forgotten that the length of a sentence depends, not on the number of its bars, but on the number of its accents and the position of its cadences.   Here, although the final chords of the cadences always come on the last beats of the bars, we have not feminine endings, because these last beats are the strong (fourth and eighth) accents.

356. The first part of this movement (to the end of bar 8) is a complete binary form (§ 352) containing two sentences, the first closing in the relative major, and the second returning to the tonic key.   The second part of the movement begins with a modulation to E flat, in which key we find the episode.   This is also made of two sentences; the first is four bars in length, ending with a full close (bar 4) with feminine ending; the second sentence is extended to five bars by the repetition of its first bar an octave higher (5a).   Its fore-phrase finishes with an interrupted cadence (bar 6), and its after-phrase with a full cadence in bar 8.   The second part is completed by a third sentence, modulating back to G minor, and ending with a half cadence in that key.   The third part is an exact repetition of the first, followed by a coda of one sentence in which four bars are extended to five by the sequential repetition of the second bar.   The final cadence has a feminine ending.

357. Our next example is rather more extended.

The form of this movement is perfectly clear. The first part is, like our last example, in binary form, each half being repeated, as we so frequently saw in the last chapter. The second sentence is extended by the addition of a new after-phrase. The middle part of the movement resembles in its form the trio of a minuet, each half being repeated. It is in itself a perfectly complete binary form, and is followed by a *codetta** of four bars, containing two full cadences over a tonic pedal. The first part of the movement is then repeated without modification, and a short coda of four bars is appended, founded upon the subject of the episode, but in the major mode.

358. It is very common to find that the episode in a ternary form will have the same tonic as the principal subject, but be in a major instead of a minor key, or *vice versa*. The andante just given illustrates this point. Another familiar example is the Andante of Beethoven's Sonata in D, Op. 28. The movement is so well known that it will suffice to remind the student that it begins with a subject in binary form (each part repeated) in D minor. The middle portion is also in binary form (D major), with repetitions, after which the first part is repeated with considerable embellishment, and a short coda concludes the movement.

359. The variation of the principal subject on its repetition in the third part of the movement is very frequently found as a feature of the ternary form. Our next illustration will show this, as well as some other points not seen in our last extracts.

Adagio cantabile.   HAYDN.   Quartett, Op. 64, No. 5.

---

* The name *codetta* (a diminutive of *coda*) is applied to passages similar in character to a coda, but introduced in the course of, instead of at the end of a movement.

In condensing this beautiful movement on two staves, though
every note of the original has been retained, some crossings of
the two middle voices have not been indicated, for the sake of
clearness.   The first part of this Adagio contains three sentences,
of which the first and second are of the normal length of eight
bars each; while the third is extended, by various prolongations
from eight bars to eighteen.   We recommend the student carefully
to examine the rhythmic analyses of all the pieces in this chapter.
One of our chief objects in giving these movements complete is
to furnish illustrations of the practical application of the general
principles given in Chapter VIII. as to the extension and contraction of phrases and sentences.

360. The second part of this movement opens in A minor,
with imitative treatment of the first bar of the principal subject.

The real episodical theme, however, is not found till the fifth bar, when it enters in C major. An examination of what follows proves very clearly that here is the beginning of an eight-bar sentence; we consequently mark this bar $(5=1)$; and we see here a sentence with an additional fore-phrase, instead of (as in so many of our earlier examples) an additional after-phrase $(8=4)$. The true episode here consists of only the one eight-bar sentence in the key of C major—a key in the second degree of relationship to the original tonic (§ 83). .The sentence is followed by a four-bar phrase returning to A minor, and ending on the dominant of that key, to lead back to the third part of the movement.

361. If the student will compare the third part with the first, he will find that not only the rhythmic, but the harmonic outlines of the two parts are absolutely identical. This third part is, in fact, nothing but a florid variation of the first part. Unlike the two movements previously given, there is here not a single bar of coda.

362. Our next illustration will be the Adagio of Beethoven's 'Sonate Pathétique.'

BEETHOVEN. Sonata, Op. 13.

Before proceeding to speak of the form of this movement, it will be advisable to say a few words concerning the marks of phrasing. The meaning of the slur as an indication of *legato* is quite familiar, and the student is generally taught that between the end of one slur and the beginning of the next there should be a break, which is effected by giving the last note under a slur rather less than its proper value. But, as a matter of fact, we scarcely ever find with the old composers (and not often even with more modern ones) that the marks of phrasing correspond to the rhythmic subdivision of the phrases and sentences. We have shown in Chapters II. and III. of this volume the underlying principles on which melody is constructed ; and it has been seen that, with rare exceptions, unaccented notes belong to the following, and not to the preceding accented note. But if we try to play this movement, attending strictly to the phrasing printed, we get the most absurd effects. The analysis of the sentences into phrases, sections and motives proves the correct phrasing to be quite different.

363. In order to make our meaning clear, we will analyze two sentences (the second and third) of this movement. We begin at the ninth bar, where the first sentence is repeated an octave higher.

An examination of the harmony of the first of these two sentences shows that the fore-phrase divides into two sections, while the after-phrase is continuous. The sequential character of bars 5 and 6 prevents our regarding the E in bar 6 as the end of a section. Here, therefore, we have an illustration of what was said in § 53. We need hardly say that the first section of the fore-phrase ends on E, not on D, which therefore ought not to be included in the first slur.

364. In the second sentence, the phrasing corresponds with the motives throughout. In order to show this more clearly, we have separated the last three semiquavers in the first three bars of this sentence from the tied semiquaver preceding them; and in bar 4 we have written out the turn in full, as it is evidently the commencement of the following motive. Of the overlapping of the phrases in this sentence we shall speak presently.

365. This volume is not intended to teach pianoforte playing, though we hope it may be found useful by pianists as well as composers; but the question of phrasing is so intimately connected with the structure of a composition, that, as the present piece furnishes a striking example of the loose and inaccurate way in which printed music is generally phrased, it gives an opportunity to warn students not to be misled, in making analyses for themselves, by finding the natural subdivision of the sentences contradicted by the position of the slurs.

366. We now come to the analysis of the form of this adagio. Many writers consider the first part of the movement to end at the sixteenth bar, after the repetition of the first sentence; and they regard the third sentence, which begins in F minor, as the first episode. In that case, as the piece would have two episodes, and, in all, three appearances of the principal subject, it would belong to one of the Rondo forms, of which we shall speak in the next volume of this series. We do not take this view, because the second sentence is only a repetition of the first, with rather fuller harmony; it is therefore analogous to the repetition of the first sentence which we saw in our example to § 357. Besides this, the third sentence is rather a continuation of, than a contrast to what has preceded. It is, in fact, the second part of a large binary form, which is completed by the repetition of its opening sentence.

367. The construction of the third sentence, which begins at the 17th bar, deserves attention. We see here an instance of the overlapping of the two phrases (§ 258), the last bar of the fore-phrase being also the first bar of the after-phrase (4 = 5). It is more common to find two sentences overlapping than two phrases, as here, of the same sentence. The end of this sentence is extended by two repetitions of the cadence, the tonic chord of the second (8b) being prolonged through two bars.

368. The second part of the movement contains only one complete sentence of eight bars, which commences in A flat minor, and modulates to E major—the enharmonic of its sub-mediant, F flat (compare the example in § 315). This sentence is followed by a passage, six bars in length, which modulates back to the original tonic. It is impossible to consider these bars as either an extended phrase or a contracted sentence, because of their want of cadential character. We have here the first example we have yet seen of what may be termed a *link*,—that is, a passage which, without forming a part of a sentence itself, connects the preceding with the following sentence. Such passages are not uncommon in large works.*

369. The third part of the movement consists of the repetition of the first sixteen bars of the first part, with a new accompaniment of triplet semiquavers. It is followed by a short coda, which (unlike the codas in the examples, §§ 355, 357) contains no new sentence or phrase, but is composed entirely of cadential repetitions, first two bars long, and then (according to a very common practice of Beethoven) diminished to half that length.

370. A movement very similar in form to that just analyzed, though of considerably larger dimensions, is the *Adagio Grazioso* of Beethoven's Sonata in G major, Op. 31, No. 1. Our space will not allow us to give the piece in full; but a short analysis of it will be of service to the student, who is recommended to number the bars of his copy for reference.

371. The first part of the movement extends to bar 34, and is in itself a complete binary form. The first two sentences are of the normal eight-bar length, the first ending with a full cadence in the tonic, and the second in the dominant key (bar 16). The third sentence (bars 16 to 26) is less regular; the two sections of which its fore-phrase is made are each extended by the insertion of an unaccented bar (bars 17 and 20), and the fore-phrase ends in bar 22. Instead of a complete after-phrase, we have in bar 23 a half cadence in C; for the F♯ in these bars is seen by its continual contradiction by F♮ to be chromatic. Cadential repetitions here take the place of the after-phrase, as is not infrequently seen

---

* Dr. Riemann has given to such passages the name of " General Auftakt," *i.e.* " general *up-beat*," using the term "up-beat" with reference to a whole sentence, in the same way in which he applies it to the unaccented part of a motive.

in a middle sentence (compare the examples in §§ 283, 285, 321). The fourth sentence (bars 27 to 34) is an ornamented repetition of the first (bars 1 to 8).

372. The second part of the movement (bars 34 to 65) commences with a modulation to A flat. The first sentence is incomplete, the first two-bar section of the fore-phrase being elided, or replaced only by the arpeggio of the chord of C minor (bars 34, 35). The full cadence in bar 41 clearly shows the end of a sentence, of which the commencement of the melody in bar 36 is obviously the third bar. The following sentence (bars 42 to 53) is extended by the addition of a second after-phrase, and the 49th bar is (8 = 4). From bars 53 to 64 we see only prolongations and repetitions of cadences—another example of the *link* (§ 368) to lead on to the third part of the movement.

373. If we compare this third part (bars 65 to 98) bar by bar with the first part (bars 1 to 34) we shall find that the melodic and harmonic outlines of the two are precisely similar. The only differences are that on its repetition the melody is more florid in its embellishments and the accompaniment for the left hand is fuller and richer. In the former respect, it resembles the Adagio by Haydn given in § 359; but in that movement the accompaniments were precisely the same in the third as in the first part of the movement. The *coda* with which the present movement concludes (bars 98 to 119) is more elaborate than those seen in the examples hitherto given. Like that in the Sonata Pathétique (§ 362), it consists entirely of repeated and extended cadences in the tonic key; these are seen at bars 103, 108, 110, 112, 113, 115, 116, 118, 119. It will be noticed that, as they are repeated, the cadences are introduced at shorter distances, according to a plan of which we have already seen other instances in Beethoven's works, and that they are formed from the first two bars of the opening theme of the movement.

374. The Adagio of Weber's first sonata gives an example of a different variety of ternary form.

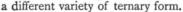

(I.) *Adagio.*   WEBER. Sonata in C, Op. 24.

The first part of this movement contains two sentences, the former being of the normal length (eight bars), while the latter, which has two fore-phrases and two after-phrases, is thereby extended to sixteen bars. This second sentence should be carefully examined, as it illustrates the possibility of introducing intermediate cadential harmonies on other bars than the fourth and eighth. The first fore-phrase of this sentence ends at (*a*) with a full cadence. We do not regard the cadence at (*b*), two bars later, as a repetition (4a) of the preceding; because from the cadence at (*a*) to the inverted cadence in D minor at (*c*) we find exactly eight bars; the passage therefore divides into two four-bar phrases, as we have marked it. At (*b*), the second bar of the new phrase, we have a stronger cadential effect than at the fourth bar; while we see again an inverted cadence in F minor at the fifth bar. Evidently, if we try to analyze the passage by considering every cadence here as indicating an accented bar, according to our usual plan, we shall have to infer so much complexity of extension or contraction of the phrases, that it is far simpler and more rational to look at the passage *as a whole*; by this means the construction of the entire sentence becomes very clear.

375. An important difference between this movement and those previously given is, that here the second (episodical) part is considerably the longest of the three—nearly as long, in fact, as the other two together. It is also most unusual for the second part of a ternary movement to begin in the key of the dominant, nor can we give any other example of it. The keys generally employed, if the movement is in a major key, will be either the subdominant, the tonic minor, or (more rarely) the relative minor,—sometimes also (as in the Adagio from Beethoven's Sonata, Op. 31, No. 1, and in the example in § 359), a key in the second degree of relationship (§ 83). That the sentence of twelve (8 + 4) bars here belongs to the second part of the movement, is proved by the fact that there is no return afterwards to the key of F. The following sentence, which begins in C minor, is also extended to twelve bars.

376. At the full cadence in D flat (*d*), a new sentence commences. The position of the next full cadence shows that there is here an elision of the first section of the fore-phrase, which we accordingly indicate by (8 = 2). As if by way of compensation, the following sentence is extended from eight bars to ten, first by the insertion of an unaccented bar (5a), and then by the repetition of the last bar. The middle part of the movement ends, as is often the case, on the dominant of the original key.

377. The construction of the last part of this movement is as curious as it is unusual. The fore-phrase of the opening theme is given three times, each time with a different harmony; after which the first two bars form the beginning of a sentence with a new continuation, leading to the cadence which concluded the first

part of the movement. Neither the whole of the first part, nor any one complete sentence of it, is repeated; but the use made of the fore-phrase shows clearly enough the ternary form of the movement, which ends with five bars of cadential repetitions over a tonic pedal.

378. It will be seen that all the movements we have yet analyzed in this chapter are slow movements from larger works. In all large compositions of several movements, such as sonatas, quartetts, or symphonies, when they are regular in construction, if the ternary form is found, it will be either in the minuet or scherzo, as already mentioned (§ 351), or in the slow movement. The first and last movements will be in other forms which will be treated of in the next volume of this series. It is true that we exceptionally meet with a ternary form in a first movement, as in Beethoven's Sonata in E flat, Op. 27, No. 1; but it must be remembered that the title the composer has given to it—'*Sonata quasi Fantasia*' shows that the work is not in the regular form. In Beethoven's Sonata in G, Op. 14, No. 2, we find the ternary form in the finale; but this is because the work (quite exceptionally) ends with a scherzo. As a general rule, the employment of this form is restricted to the middle movements of larger works.

379. As an independent form—that is, for pieces which are complete in one movement—the ternary form is even more common than as a part of a larger work. A very large number of modern pianoforte pieces (Caprices, Nocturnes, Impromptus, &c.) are written in this form; indeed it may be said that the majority of so-called '*Morceaux de Salon*,' when they exceed the limits of the simple binary form, will be found to be ternary in construction. We shall now give a few examples of this form, analyzing them rhythmically, as in previous cases.

380. Our first illustration will be one of the shorter Nocturnes of Chopin.

This movement is remarkably clear in its construction and its
analysis offers not the slightest difficulty of any kind.   With the

exception of the link of two bars introduced between the end of
the second and the beginning of the third part, there is no
rhythmic irregularity at all.   Every sentence throughout the
piece is of the normal length of eight bars ; there is neither
extension, contraction, or overlapping, with the solitary exception
of the repetition of the final cadence.   It is rare to find such
rhythmic uniformity in a piece of this length ; and the student
should notice how carefully Chopin has avoided monotony by
varying his cadences.

381. The first part of the movement contains five eight-bar
sentences, of which the fourth and fifth are repetitions of the
second and third, with a little more ornamentation.   The episode,
in E flat, contains three sentences, the third leading back toward
the original key, of which the chord of C minor is, of course, the
subdominant.   Two bars of link introduce the third part, which
is the same as the first, with the omission of the two repeated
sentences.

382. Our next example offers considerably more material for
comment.

This movement begins with an eight-bar sentence, ending with a full close in the tonic, and twice repeated with unimportant modifications. The following sentence modulates through G flat to E flat minor; and at (*a*) the sentence is extended by three bars. We have here an instance of overlapping by the conversion of an accented into an unaccented bar (8 = 5). The next sentence is in the key of G flat throughout, and is followed by a link, leading back to the first subject. Though this link is eight bars in length, we cannot consider it as a sentence, for it has no cadence, and consists simply of the chord of the dominant minor ninth of E flat. The first theme of the movement is then repeated; but its continuation is varied, the second sentence being extended from eight bars to twelve, and ending in the tonic. *minor*, in which key the first part of the piece closes, after several cadential extensions and repetitions.

383. A short link connects the final cadence of the first part with the second, which begins in the remote key of B minor (the enharmonic of C flat, the submediant of E flat minor). The introduction of the major key of the submediant for the middle part of a ternary form is very common, but that of the submediant *minor* (as here) is extremely rare.

384. The rhythmic analysis of this middle division of the movement is very instructive. Notice at (*b*) that we mark (8 = 4) instead of marking the bar as (8) and the cadence four bars later

P

as 8a because there is no full close at (*b*). When the full
cadence is reached, it is twice repeated (8a, 8b). At (*c*) it is
evidently a second fore-phrase (the transposition of the preceding
one a fourth higher), and not an after-phrase, that begins ; the bar
is therefore (5 = 1) ; and the second section of this fore-phrase is
then twice repeated in a varied form (4a, 4b).

385. At (*d*) begins a link of considerable extent to introduce
the third part of the movement. Notice in the bars immediately
preceding the link an example of the cross accents spoken of in
§ 287. The third part of the movement is an exact repetition of
the first, and is followed by a coda in which the keys of B (C flat)
minor and E flat minor are brought into close juxtaposition with a
very curious and original effect. After the explanations already
given, the rhythmic analysis of this coda will offer no difficulty to
the student. Observe that the movement ends on an unaccented
bar,—that is, with a feminine ending.

386. Schumann's pianoforte pieces afford many examples of
the ternary form. We select for our next illustration the well-
known 'Aufschwung' from the 'Phantasiestücke,' Op. 12, not
only because it shows a variety of form that we have not yet met
with, but because its rhythmic analysis is somewhat difficult, and
the explanation of the same will be helpful to the student.

* '' Sehr rasch'' (*German*)=very fast.

387. Many analysts would consider the first subject of this piece to end at the sixteenth bar, and would regard the passage in D flat which follows as forming the first episode. In that case the piece would be a Rondo, containing, as will be seen, three episodes, and four appearances of the principal subject. We do not consider this to be the correct analysis of its form, because the chief subject would only contain one sentence (which is repeated) and would end, at the sixteenth bar, in a key other than the tonic of the piece. It is much simpler to keep consistently to the principles enunciated in § 352, and to regard this movement as beginning with an extended binary form. From this point of view the first part of the movement contains six sentences. The first (of which the second is a repetition) begins in F minor, and ends with a full cadence in A flat, the relative major. The three sentences that follow, beginning and ending in the key of D flat, have, it must be admitted, an episodical character, in so far as that they are in contrast with what has preceded ; but we consider them nevertheless to belong to the first part of the movement because they have not been preceded by a full close in the tonic key. The first theme is then repeated, and modified,—first by

the repetition of its fore-phrase in the key of B flat minor (the subdominant) and then by such an alteration of the after-phrase as will enable it to end in F minor.

388. Up to this point the rhythmic structure of this movement has been quite regular and symmetrical ; the only departure from the normal form has been the insertion of an additional fore-phrase in the last sentence. In the second part, which we are now to examine, the rhythms are much more complex,—so much so, indeed, that the analysis of the passage requires to be carefully reasoned out, step by step. The first eight-bar sentence is quite regular, with a feminine ending, as also is the following phrase of four bars ; but from this point the complications begin.

389. If we count onward four bars from (*a*) we find a third inversion of a fundamental ninth, which cannot possibly be the end of a sentence. But if we look at the third bar from (*a*) we see in it the tonic chord of E flat, preceded in the bar before by the dominant harmony of the same key, the real notation of the passage being

Here we clearly see a cadence in E flat ; we know, therefore, that the sentence ends here, as we have already seen that it cannot end in the next bar. Counting back from this point, we see that the after-phrase has an elision of the fifth (an unaccented) bar. Two bars later the cadence is repeated (8a).

390. The next sentence is also complicated in its rhythm. The bar at (*b*) is evidently an accented bar because of the decided change of harmony in it (§ 208) ; this is therefore a fourth bar, marking the end of a fore-phrase. Two sequential repetitions (4a, 4b) of this fore-phrase follow. It looks at first as if the bar which we have marked (6) should be marked (4c = 6). We have not so indicated it, because the resemblance to what has preceded is hardly sufficiently close. It is quite clear that the two bars *ritenuto* here lead up to the close of the sentence, on the last (eighth) bar of which the opening subject of the second part of the movement is repeated. After an eight-bar sentence with feminine ending, as before, a passage of irregular construction, 22 bars in length, leads back to the first subject, and the third part of the piece. The passage in question begins at (*c*) ; and an examination of the harmony shows us that here we have again an elision of the first unaccented bar. The fore-phrase is twice repeated, and is followed by a link of ten bars, which does duty instead of an after-phrase. The entire absence of cadences

renders it impossible to regard this link as forming any part of a sentence.

391. The third part of this movement is again perfectly regular in its construction. It resembles the first part, but is somewhat compressed, and its middle portion is now transposed from D flat to A flat. The final sentence, also, is not extended as before, and its after-phrase is somewhat altered. It will be seen that the piece contains no coda.

392. Like the binary form treated of in our last chapter, the ternary form is also used in vocal music, though more frequently by composers of the last century than by those of the present day. With Handel and Bach, the former especially, we find numerous examples, both in sacred and secular music. The most common form is that of the air with a second part (usually in the relative minor if the movement is in a major key, and in the relative major if it is in a minor one), after which the whole first part is repeated *Da Capo*—that is, from the beginning. As a short example of this form we give the beautiful song "Qual nave smarrita" from Handel's opera 'Radamisto.'

393. The first part of this air is a perfectly clear binary form, which evidently divides naturally into two parts. The former of these contains two sentences, the first, of eight bars, for orchestra alone, ending in the key of the tonic; while the second, in which the voice enters, is extended by an additional after-phrase to twelve bars, and closes in the key of the dominant. The second part begins with the fore-phrase of the opening symphony, given, as before, to the orchestra, to which a new after-phrase is added for the voice. The following sentence is extended to ten bars by a sequential repetition (4a) of the second section of the fore-phrase. The next sentence is incomplete, the first section of the fore-phrase being elided. We might consider this passage as a continuation of the last sentence, as its after-phrase is so similar; but it is better here to regard it as a new sentence, because it seems (so to speak) to make a fresh start after the full cadence in the tonic key with which the preceding sentence closed. The concluding symphony of four bars for the orchestra is so evidently cadential in feeling and character that we look upon it simply as a strengthening of the last cadence, and therefore mark the last bar as (8a). The second part of this air consists of only one sentence of twelve bars, after which the whole of the first part (now become the third) is repeated.

394. In airs constructed on this plan, both parts are often far more extended than in the example just analyzed. As very familiar instances, may be cited the airs "He was despised" in the 'Messiah,' and "Honour and arms" in 'Samson.' Many other songs of similar form will occur to the memory of the student who is acquainted with Handel's oratorios.

395. Exceptionally we meet with movements which it is difficult to consider as in any but ternary form, in which the first

part ends in the key of the dominant, instead of in the tonic. A striking example of this is the song "Why does the God of Israel sleep?" in 'Samson,' which, unfortunately, is far too long to quote here. The key of the piece is B flat; the first part of the song contains 43 bars, and ends in the key of F major. The second part, 32 bars in length, begins in G minor, and passes through C minor to D minor, in which key it concludes. The third part contains 42 bars, and is formed from the same material as the first, but with considerable variety of treatment; it ends, of course, in the tonic key.

396. The song of which we are now speaking furnishes an illustration of the difficulty which is sometimes met with in exactly defining the form of a movement. We can hardly regard a piece of the length of 117 bars as being in simple binary form; but, on the other hand, when carefully examined, this air fails to satisfy either of the essential conditions we have laid down as characterizing the ternary form. Not only does the first part not end in the tonic key, but in the second part, though the keys employed are just those which Handel would have selected for the middle portion of a song in B flat with a '*Da Capo*,' the thematic material is the same as that of the first part. The piece is, in fact, a compromise between the binary and ternary form, and is an example of the "mixed forms" of which we shall have more to say in the next volume.

397. Of the more modern employment of the ternary form in vocal music two excellent examples will be found in Beethoven's songs 'An die Hoffnung' (Op. 94)* and 'Lied aus der Ferne.' The form is also not infrequent in our English ballads, in which, when the poem contains three stanzas, the first and third are set to the same music, while the second is different.

398. Sometimes the middle portion of a ternary movement will be in a different tempo from the first and third parts. This is the case in Beethoven's 'Lied aus der Ferne,' just referred to, where the middle part is in $\frac{2}{4}$ time, while the first and third parts are in $\frac{6}{8}$. A fine instance will also be seen in Handel's 'Alcina.' The first part of the air "Ah, mio cor! schernito sei!" is an *andante larghetto* ($\frac{3}{4}$ time), in C minor, in which the enchantress bewails her desertion by her lover; but when, in the second part of the air she summons up her courage and vows vengeance ("Ma che fà gemendo Alcina?") the time changes to *allegro* (C) with an animated semiquaver figure for the violins, after which the first part is repeated.

399. A better known instance of a change of time for the

---

* Beethoven wrote two songs to these words; it is the second, and longer setting which is here referred to.

second part of a ternary movement is furnished by the scherzo of Beethoven's Choral Symphony, in which the scherzo is in $\frac{3}{4}$ and the trio in ₵ time. Another example, perhaps even more striking, will be seen in the scherzo of Schubert's string quintett, Op. 163. The scherzo itself is *presto*, $\frac{3}{4}$, and the trio *andante sostenuto*, ₵.

400. It will be seen, from the numerous examples that we have analyzed or referred to in this chapter, that the ternary form is so elastic, and capable of such endless modifications of detail, that it is quite beyond the limits of such a volume as this to give an exhaustive description of its possibilities. Enough has, however, been said, to enable the student to recognize it without difficulty, and to compose pieces in this form if he wishes to do so. The general outline will be always the same :—

First Part:—A short piece in binary form, containing two or more sentences, and ending in the key of the tonic.

Second Part:—An episode in a different key from the first part,* made from new subjects, which should be contrasted with, rather than a continuation of, those in the first part. The second part may be either a complete binary form (see example § 357), or its last sentence may lead back to the dominant of the original key.

Third Part:—The repetition of the first part, entirely or partially, with or without variation or embellishment. A *coda* may be added if desired.

401. We have now followed the growth and development of musical forms from their simplest origin. We have seen how from the combination of motives we obtain in turn sections, phrases, and sentences. The laws of rhythm have been examined, and the nature of irregular, as well as of regular sentences explained. It has been shown how two or more sentences can be combined to make the simple binary form ; and lastly, we have dealt with the further extension of the binary to a ternary form. At this point the first part of our task is completed. These two forms are the only *typical* forms existing in music. Yet it must not be supposed that they are always to be found in the comparatively simple shape in which we have been studying them in this volume. In instrumental music we frequently meet (and in vocal music, though to a less extent) with pieces which certainly cannot be analyzed as belonging to either the simple binary or ternary form. It is important for the student to realize the fact that, just as we saw in Chapter VIII. that all sentences and phrases of irregular rhythm are variations of the normal rhythm of four and eight bars, so all the larger forms—the sonata, rondo,

---

* Except occasionally in a Minuet and Trio, where it is *possible* (though seldom advisable) for the Trio to be in the same key as the Minuet.

variation, &c.—are either extensions or varieties of one of the
two typical forms described and explained in this and the preceding chapter.   Such forms are appropriately termed APPLIED
FORMS.   Their nature and treatment will form the subject of our
next volume; and it will be found that the organic growth of
which we have several times spoken in the present work will still
be traceable in the larger and more complicated forms which have
yet to be examined.   The deeper the insight which the student
obtains into the fundamental principles of musical structure, the
more thorough will be his appreciation, and the richer his enjoyment of the artistic symmetry which underlies the masterpieces
of the great composers.

ANALYTICAL INDEX.

Accent in poetry and verse, 19, 20, 21.
Accented bar, cadence in, 39, 74 (VI.).
ACCENTED BAR interpolated, in a phrase, 242; almost invariably in after-phrase—why, 242; in both fore- and after-phrase, producing regular five-bar rhythm, 245, 246.
ACCENTED BEAT, elision of, in a bar, 299; harmony to be changed on, 208; interpolation of, in a bar, 295-297.
Accented note, preceded by unaccented note, the simplest form of the motive, 59.
ACCENTED AND UNACCENTED bars, 38, 39, 74 (VI.), 185; how to determine, 39-41, 74 (VI.); in two-bar motives, 73; notes, 59, 60; phrases, 50.
Accompaniment, establishing a figure of, 265.
After-phrase and fore-phrase, 50.
Ambiguous chords in modulation, 107, 110.
ANALOGY between music and poetry, 18, 22; music and prose, 22.
Anglican chant, an example of the elision of an unaccented bar, 250.
Anticipation of harmony on unaccented beat or bar, 209.
Antithesis and thesis, 26.
Arpeggios and broken chords occurring in a melody—implied harmony of, 13.
Attendant keys, 81.
Augmented sixth, chord of, used in enharmonic modulation, 144-150.

Balance an essential of musical form, 10, 26.
Bar in which a cadence occurs is always

an accented bar (except sometimes with feminine endings), 39, 74 (VI.).
Barring, incorrect, example of, 37.
BARS, accented and unaccented, 38, 39, 74 (VI.), 185; how to determine, 39-41, 74 (VI.).
BINARY FORM defined, 306; possibility of contracting and extending sentences, 307; sometimes called "two-part song form," or "lied form," 337; symmetry and contrast, 307.
I. SIMPLEST BINARY FORM, consisting of two complete sentences, 306, 308; examples, 308, 309; prolongation of a cadence, 309.
II. THE CONCISE BINARY FORM, consisting of two sentences, 310; (*a*) found mostly in simple songs, dances, and themes for variations, 310; (*b*) as an independent form, 310; example by Schumann analyzed, 310; remote modulation in, 310; another example by Schumann, 311; modulation to nearly related keys, 311; thematic material examined, 312; gavotte by Corelli analyzed, 313; minuet and trio by Mozart analyzed, 314; waltz by Schubert analyzed, 315; modulation to key in second degree of relationship, 315; theme for variations by Haydn analyzed, 316; contredanse by Beethoven analyzed, 317; first eight bars ending with a half cadence explained, 317.
III. CONCISE BINARY FORM IN VOCAL MUSIC, 318; examples quoted, 318; modulations to nearly related keys, 318; strophic song by

Q

Weber analyzed, 319; song by Mozart analyzed, 320; commencing with end of a sentence, 320; repetition of final cadence, 320.

IV. EXTENDED BINARY FORM, sentences of irregular construction, 321; absolute uniformity of rhythm not often maintained for more than 16 bars except in the smallest forms, 321; example by Haydn analyzed, 321; sentence prolonged by repetition of cadence, 322; gavotte by Bach analyzed, 323; consisting of three sentences, 323; regularity of cadences in—why, 324; modulations, 324; thematic material examined, 325; treatment of the motive, 325; minuet by Handel analyzed, 326; consisting of five sentences, 326; extension of last sentence by repetition of its after-phrase, 326; bourrée by Bach analyzed, 327; consisting of four sentences, 327.

V. EXTENDED BINARY FORM IN VOCAL MUSIC, 328; cavatinas mostly written in this form, 328; use of this form by Handel in oratorio and opera, 328; example by Handel analyzed, 328, 329; commencing in the middle of a sentence, 328; the regularity of its form, 328; the time in—unit of measurement, 329.

VI. BINARY FORM WITH TWO SUBJECTS, 330; second subject in a different key to the first, 330; this form the germ out of which modern sonata form has been developed, 336; its great importance, 336; prelude by Bach analyzed, 331, 332; second subject on repetition appearing in key of tonic, 332; example by Mozart analyzed, 333-335.

BINARY AND TERNARY forms the only typical forms existing in music, 401

Bourrée by Bach as an example of extended binary form, 327.

Broken chords and arpeggios occurring in a melody—implied harmony, 13.

CADENCE, an element of musical form, 9; at the end of *sections,* 55, 56, 74 (IV.); at the end of *phrases,* 29-31, 74 (III.), 186; at the end of *sentences,* 24, 74 (II.); at the end of phrases and sentences always in accented bar (except sometimes with feminine endings), 39; feminine endings explained, 28, 37; in poetry and prose, 19-21; lengthening last notes of, 223; middle, 29-31, 74 (III.), 186; prolongation of final, 222, 224; prolongation of, in both fore- and after-phrase, 229; repetition of, 222, 320-322; repetition of, a common practice with Beethoven, 369; repetition of, with extension, 227; repetition of, with variation, 228; regularity of, in dance music and small compositions, 10.

Cadential harmonies, intermediate, 374.

Cavatinas mostly written in binary form, 328.

CHANGE OF HARMONY on accented beat, 208; on accented note of motive, 208.

Choice of keys to modulate to, 168, 324, 339, 346.

Chord of the seventh in enharmonic modulation, 144-150.

Chord of the minor ninth in enharmonic modulation, 139-142.

CHORD OF THE MINOR THIRTEENTH in enharmonic modulation, 151-153; modulation to 18 keys by, 151.

Chord of the augmented sixth in enharmonic modulation, 144-150.

CHORDS, COMMON, to two keys—key relationship, 80-83; to two keys, modulation by — (*see* Modulation, Means of); to nearly related keys, 80-83; to keys in second degree of relationship, 83-86.

Chords in final cadence, position of, 37, 40.

CHROMATIC modulation, 161-167; scale used as a means of modulation, 158; notation of, 158; triads used as a means of modulation, 112-128.

Coda and Codetta, difference between, 357 (note).

CODA defined, 352; examples, 355-357, 369, 373.

CODETTA defined, 357; example, 357.

Complex rhythms in polyphonic music, 269.

COMPOSITION, hints for first attempts in, 338-347; *how to write hymn tunes,* 339-343; modulation, 339; outlines to be filled up, 341; sequential passages, 340; variety of cadence, 339;

paraphrasing defined, 344; example of, 344; *short pieces, how to write,* of two, three, and four sentences, 345, 346; modulation—the subdominant key, 346; sentences of irregular length, 347.

COMPOUND modulation defined, 159; example of, 146, 159; time, German definition of, 36.

Concise binary form (*see* Binary Form).

Contraction and extension of sentences (*see* Irregular Rhythms).

Contrasted motives, 183.

Contredanse by Beethoven as an example of concise binary form, 317.

CROSS ACCENTS, 287-293, 296, 385.

Crossing the bar accent and rhythmic accent, 287.

DANCE MUSIC, binary form in, 310; uniformity of rhythm in, 321, 323.

Development defined, variety of, 12.

Diatonic scale used as a means of modulation, 157.

Diatonic sevenths used as a means of modulation, 133-137.

Diatonic triads used as a means of modulation, 102-111.

Different views of theorists on the subject of form, 349.

Diminished seventh used in enharmonic modulation to connect *any* two keys, 139.

Diminished triad used as a means of modulation, 132.

Disguised motives, 181, 182.

Distinction between poetry and prose, 19, 20.

Dotted bars, use of, in irregular compound times, 301, 303.

Eight- and sixteen- bar sentences, the normal form, 220.

Eight-bar rhythm defined, 9.

Eight-bar sentences, how to construct (*see* Regular Rhythm).

ELISION of a beat in a bar, 299; of unaccented part of a motive, 60; of accented bar cannot be effected, 258; of unaccented smaller, 248-255; of a section, 267, 332, 372, 376, 393; of a phrase, 268, 328; of a whole sentence excepting the final bar, 266, 279, 320, 392.

ENHARMONIC MODULATION by chord of fundamental seventh, 144-147; by chord of minor ninth (diminished seventh), 139-143; by chord of minor thirteenth, 151-153; by chord of augmented sixth, 144-150; notation of key approached mostly used, 98, 140-143.

Enharmonic modulation—Implied, 86.

EPISODE IN TERNARY FORM—an essential element, 350; defined, 350, 400; form of, 352; keys for and examples of, 352, 356, 358-360, 375, 380; in vocal music, 392; time sometimes changed for, 398, 399.

Every regular musical sentence, or part of a sentence, is made up of an alternation of accented and unaccented bars —exceptions, 38.

Extended binary form (*see* Binary Form).

Extension and contraction of sentences, the reason for, 221.

Extension of sentences (*see* Irregular Rhythms).

Extreme modulations (*see* Modulation, Means of).

Fantasia, defined, form underlying, 4.

FEMININE ENDING defined, 28; examples of, 28, 33, 34, 43, 45, 46, 56; very common both in phrases and sentences, 28.

Figure of accompaniment, establishing, 265.

Figure, rhythmic, 180, 210.

Five-bar rhythm (*see* Irregular Rhythms).

Foot defined, 21.

Fore-phrase, cadences in, 186.

Fore-phrase and after-phrase, 50.

FORM, binary (*see* Binary Form); cadence in, 9; defined, 2; development, 12; essentials of, 5; melody in, 6; melody and harmony, their intimate connection, 13; modulation in, 11; proportion in, 10; rhythm in, 9; sonata, developed from the binary form with two subjects, 336; ternary (*see* Ternary Form); tonality in, 7.

Forms, the larger, developed from the smaller, 307.

Formula for indicating the subdivisions of sentences, 188.

Four- and eight-bar phrases and sentences the basis of all musical forms, 221.

Four-bar sentences, their construction
explained, 30, 184, 197, 313 319.
Full cadence, how to avoid the feeling of
finality in, 29, 33, 35.
FUGUE, analysis of fugue by Bach,
270-276 ; irregular rhythms in, 277.
Fugues, regularity of accent often supplies
the place of regular rhythm in—why,
277, 278.
Fundamental discords used as a means of
modulation (*see* Modulation, Means
of).

GAVOTTE by Corelli, as an example of
concise binary form, 313; by Bach, as
an example of *extended* binary form,
323-325.
German definition of compound time,
36.
German sixth the only form of the chord
of the augmented sixth available in
enharmonic modulation, 144.

Harmony and melody, connection between, 13, 14.
HARMONY, anticipation of, on unaccented
beat or bar, 208, 209 ; arpeggios and
broken chords, 13 ; extreme chromatic,
use of, 168 ; implied in a melody, 13 ;
of accented bar continued through
unaccented bar, 209 ; to be changed
on accented beat, 208.
Haydn's quartetts an exhaustless mine of
varied rhythms, 228.
How to avoid the feeling of finality in a
full cadence, 29, 33, 35.
HYMN-TUNE, construction of, analyzed,
50-52, 61 ; "Dundee," as an example
of the simplest binary form, 308 ;
hints for composing, 339-342 ; outlines
of, 341.

IMPLIED HARMONY in a melody, 13 ;
in unison passages, 44.
Implied enharmonic modulation, 86.
Impromptu by Schubert as an example
of ternary form, 382-385.
Incomplete motive, 60.
Incorrect barring, example of, 37.
Incorrect phrasing, 362-365.
INTERPOLATION of accented bar (*see* Ir-
regular Rhythms) ; of a beat in a bar,
295-297 ; of unaccented bar (*see*
Irregular Rhythms).

Intermediate cadential harmonies, 374.
IRREGULAR RHYTHMS, are not new
forms but variations of the normal four-
and eight-bar rhythms, 221; defined,
74 (1.), 221 ; essential difference between regular and irregular rhythms,
74 (1.); hints to the student, 305 ;
how to determine with accuracy the
form of sentences of irregular construction, 262 ; mostly more effective
and usual in larger than in smaller compositions, 286 ; regularity of accent
often supplies the place of regularity of
rhythm in fugues—why, 277, 278.
IRREGULAR RHYTHMS, HOW PRODUCED.

*I. PROLONGATION OF SENT-
ENCES,* by insertion of one or more
bars, 221 ; (*a*) by repetition of its
final chord, example, 222 ; (*b*) by
lengthening last chords of a cadence,
making one bar into two, example,
223 ; (*c*) by repetition and prolongation of final cadence, 224-226 ; example
by Mozart, 224 ; how to indicate such
repetitions, 225 ; two unaccented bars
between two accented bars, 224, 226,
238; example by Beethoven, cadence
with feminine ending, 227 ; (*d*) by repetition and variation of final cadence,
example by Haydn, 228 ; (*e*) by prolongation of cadence in both fore- and
after-phrase, example by Haydn, 229 ;
six-bar rhythm, example by Haydn,
230 ; (*f*) by prolongation of the *commencement* of a phrase or sentence,
232 ; extension of first bar into two
in both phrases producing *five-bar
rhythm,* example by Mozart, 232 ;
(*g*) by interpolation of one or more
bars in the *middle* of a sentence, 233 ;
example by Mozart, 233 ; repetition of
a section in the middle of a sentence,
233 ; example by Mendelssohn, 234 ;
a sentence greatly prolonged, explanation, 234-236 ; (*h*) by interpolation of
an *unaccented* bar *in the middle* of a
phrase, 238 ; example by Mozart, 238 ;
example by Mendelssohn, 239 ; an
unaccented bar repeated, 239 ; (*i*) by
insertion of unaccented bar in both
phrases producing *regular five-bar
rhythm,* 240 ; example by Schubert,
240 ; the bar usually inserted on approaching a cadence, 241 ; (*j*) by

insertion of *accented* bar in the middle of a phrase, 242 ; when only one bar is inserted it will almost invariably be in after-phrase—why, 242; example by Haydn, 242 ; example by Mendelssohn, 243 ; an accented bar repeated, 243 ; the added bar sequentially repeated, 244 ; (*k*) by insertion of accented bar in both phrases producing *regular five-bar rhythm*, 245 ; example by Schubert, 245 ; example by Prout, 246.

II. CONTRACTION OF SENTENCES, by elision of one or more bars, or by the overlapping of phrases, 221 ; (*a*) by elision of an unaccented bar, 248 ; effect of elision of first bar of a sentence, 249 ; example by Mozart, 248 ; example of an Anglican chant, 250 ; how to determine which bar has been elided, 248 ; (*b*) by elision of an intermediate bar, 251 ; examples by Mendelssohn, 251, 252 ; how to distinguish between the elision of an unaccented, and the interpolation of an accented bar, 253 ; (*c*) by elision of an unaccented bar in both phrases producing *three-bar rhythm*, 254 ; example by Haydn, 254 ; example of old Scotch, 255 ; example of Hungarian air, 255 ; example by Prout, 256 ; reason of the satisfactory effect of three-bar rhythm, 256 ; " Ritmo di tre battute," in Beethoven's Ninth Symphony, explained, 257 ; (*d*) by overlapping of two phrases or sentences, explanation of, 258 ; contraction cannot be effected by the elision of an accented bar—nearest approach to this, 258 ; example by Dussek, 259 ; example by Schumann, 260 ; example by Mendelssohn, 261 ; (*e*) by elision of *one* unaccented bar in an eight-bar sentence or phrase, producing *seven-bar rhythm*, 262 ; example by Beethoven, 262, 263 ; example by Mozart, 264 ; example of a seven-bar phrase made by extension from a four-bar phrase, 244.

III. IRREGULAR COMMENCEMENT OF SENTENCES, (*a*) first bar establishing a figure of accompaniment, example by Haydn, 265 ; (*b*)

beginning in the middle of a sentence, 266 ; beginning with a full cadence, 267 ; elision of first part of a sentence, 266 ; elision of unaccented section, 267 ; elision of unaccented phrase, 268.

IV. COMPLEX RHYTHMS OF POLYPHONIC MUSIC, 269; fugue by Bach analyzed, 270-278 ; regularity of accent frequently takes the place of regularity of rhythm, 277, 278.

V. EXAMPLES OF IRREGULAR RHYTHMS analyzed—by Haydn, 279, 280 ; by Schubert, 281, 282 ; by Mozart, 283, 284 ; by Haydn, 285, 286.

VI. CROSS ACCENTS, 287-293 ; defined, 287 ; crossing of the bar accent and the rhythmic accent, 287 ; effect of augmentation by, 293 ; example by Handel, 293 ; example by Schumann, 296 ; example by Schubert, 385 ; grouping notes of duple and quadruple time to produce the effect of triple time, 287 ; examples, 290-292 ; grouping notes of triple time to produce the effect of duple time, 287-289 ; syncopation, 287.

VII. INSERTION OF ONE BEAT IN A BAR, (*a*) in triple time, example by Handel, 295 ; in triple time, example by Schumann, 296 ; (*b*) in quadruple time, example by Mendelssohn, 297 ; (*c*) change in the subdivision of the bar, 298.

VIII. ELISION OF ONE BEAT IN A BAR, example by Schumann, 299 ; example by Dvořàk, 299.

IX. IRREGULAR COMPOUND TIMES, (*a*) *quintuple* time defined, 300 ; example by Handel, 300 ; example by Boieldieu, 301 ; use of dotted bars, 301 ; example by Chopin, 302 ; (*b*) *septuple* time defined, 300 ; example by Liszt, 303 ; use of dotted bars, 303 ; example by Berlioz, 304.

KEY RELATIONSHIP, attendant keys, 81 ; chords common to two keys, 80-83 ; defined, 80 ; key of dominant minor not included among the related keys to a major key—why, 92 ; key of subdominant major not included among the related keys to a minor key—why, 92; major keys whose tonics are consonant to one another are said to be related, 80; major keys whose tonics are dissonant to one another are unrelated, 93; minor keys are less closely related to one another than major keys, 88, 93; nearness of relationship depends upon the number of chords two keys have in common, 81-83; no single chord can define a key, 77, 160.

I. NEARLY RELATED KEYS, relationship defined, 80-82; (a) to a major key, 80, 81; table of nearly related keys, 94 (a); (b) to a minor key, 82; table of nearly related keys, 94 (a).

II. KEYS IN THE SECOND DEGREE OF RELATIONSHIP, the relationship defined, 83; (a) to a major key, connection between, 83-87; chords common to such keys, 84, 85; chromatic triads, use of, 84, 85; implied enharmonic modulation, 86; relative minors, rule, 87; tonic minor key, 87; table of keys in second degree of relationship, 94 (b); (b) to a minor key, defined, 88-90; table of keys in second degree of relationship, 94 (b).

III. UNRELATED KEYS, definition of, 93.

KEYS, choice of, for modulation in composition, 168, 324, 339, 346.

Lengthening the last notes of a cadence (*see* Irregular Rhythms).
Lied-form (binary form), 337.
LINK, defined, 368; examples of, 368, 372, 380, 382-385, 390.

MAJOR KEYS, table of nearly related, 94 (a); table of, related in the second degree, 94 (b).
Melodic form of the motive, 172.
Melody, defined, 6.
Melody and harmony, connection between, 13, 14.
Melody and rhythm, inseparable, 9
Middle cadences at end of phrases, 29-31, 74 (III), 186.
MINOR KEYS more loosely related to each

other than major keys, 88; table of nearly related, 94 (a); table of, related in the second degree, 94 (b).

MINUET by Mozart, as an example of binary form, 314; by Haydn, as an example of extended binary form, 321; by Handel, as an example of extended binary form, 326.
Mixed forms, 395, 396.
Modern sonata form—its origin, 336.
MODULATION, a constituent of musical form, 11; ambiguous chords in, 107, 110; at end of phrases, 32, 33; at end of sentences, 34, 35; compound (*see* Modulation, Means of); choice of keys for, 168, 324, 339, 346; definition of, 77; enharmonic (*see* Modulation, Means of); exercises in, 169; hints concerning, 168, 169, 324, 339, 346; importance of a thorough knowledge of, 76; in construction of short sentences, 170; in small forms, should never be made twice to the same key, 324; in short pieces, 11; means of, almost exhaustless, 95; no single chord can define a key, 77, 160; order of, 170, 346; point of, use of the motive in determining, 79, 160; to subdominant key, care required in, 346; transient, or transition, 77; to nearly related keys (*see* Modulation, Means of); to keys in the second degree of relationship (*see* Modulation, Means of); to unrelated keys (*see* Modulation, Means of).

MODULATION, MEANS OF.
I. BY CHORDS COMMON TO TWO KEYS, 96; (a) from major keys to nearly related keys, 96-99; (b) from minor keys to nearly related keys, 100-102.

II. BY MEANS OF TRIADS ONLY, 102; (a) major triads, 103; from major keys to nearly related keys, 103, 104 (a), 105 (a), 106; from minor keys to nearly related keys, 104 (b), 105 (b), 106 (b); (b) minor triads, 108; from major keys to nearly related keys, 109; from minor keys to nearly related keys, 109; to unrelated key, 111.

III. BY MEANS OF CHROMATIC TRIADS, 112, 113; (a) to keys in the second degree of relationship, 115;

to major key of mediant, 116; example by Beethoven, 121; to flat submediant major, 118; example by Brahms, 123; to submediant major, 119 (*a, b*); example by Schubert, 122; to flat mediant major, 119 (*c*); (*b*) to unrelated keys, example by Beethoven, F sharp minor to C major, 124; by Schubert, B flat to A major, 125; by Schubert, B flat to A flat major, 126; by Dvorák, B flat minor to C major, 127; extreme modulations, 114.

IV. BY MEANS OF FUNDAMENTAL DISCORDS, 129, 130; (*a*) by fundamental chords of the seventh, 131; to nearly related keys, 131; to unrelated keys, 131; example by Wagner, 131; (*b*) by diminished triad, 130, 132; taken as part of chord of seventh, and quitted as part of chord of minor ninth, 132; example by Mendelssohn, 132; (*c*) by diatonic sevenths, 133; available forms of, 133; examples by Bach, 134, 135; by Mendelssohn, 136, 137; (*d*) by chords of the major ninth, 138; example by Mendelssohn, 138 (*a*); by Bach, 138 (*b*); (*e*) by chords of the minor ninth (diminished seventh), 139; by enharmonic change of notation to every major or minor key, 139; notation of key approached mostly used, 98, 140-143; examples, 140-143; (*f*) by chord of augmented sixth, 144; by enharmonic change of notation, 144; augmented sixth on minor sixth mostly used—why, 148; German sixth the only form available, 144; dominant seventh enharmonically changed to augmented sixth, 144; examples, 145-147; augmented sixth changed to dominant seventh, 148; example by Schubert, 148; tonic seventh changed to augmented sixth, 149; example by Beethoven, 149; dominant thirteenth changed to augmented sixth, example by Beethoven, 150; (*g*) by chords of the minor thirteenth, 151; by enharmonic change of notation to 18 keys, 152; form of the chord available, 151; example by Schumann, 152; by Prout, 153.

V. BY VARIOUS OTHER MEANS, (*a*) without a connecting chord, 154 between nearly related keys mostly, 154 ; how effected, 154; implied enharmonic change possible, 155; examples, 155; (*b*) by a note common to two chords, 156; example by Beethoven, 156; (*c*) by unison passages, 156; (*d*) by diatonic or chromatic scale passages, 157; examples by Schubert, 157, 158; (*e*) by compound modulation, 159; example by Schubert, 159; (*f*) by less frequent methods, 161-166.

MOTIVE, THE, accented and unaccented notes in, 59, 60; apparently incorrect progressions explained by, 64, 65; change of harmony on accented note of, 208; *consisting of two notes,* 58-61; *consisting of more than two notes,* 62-69; with feminine endings, 63, 64; *consisting of two bars,* 70, 71; with feminine endings, 70, 72; accented and unaccented bars, 73; constituents of, 73; contrasted motives, 183; defined, 73, 74 (IV.), 58, 59, 69; disguised motives, 181, 182; elision of unaccented part of, 60; feminine endings in, 63, 64, 70, 74 (V.); general principle affecting form of, 59; importance of harmonic considerations, 64; incomplete motive, 60, 61, 74 (V.); melodic form of, 172; motives of different lengths going on simultaneously, 71; must consist of at least two notes, 60; no single note can form a motive, 71; notes of, may vary in pitch, duration, and in accent, 73; phrases commencing with complete motive, 62, 64; phrases commencing with incomplete motives, 60, 61, 63; rhythmic figure, 180; sentences constructed from, 177; simplest form of, 59, 172; sub-motives, 67, 73; treatment of, in gavotte by Bach, 325; typical motive, 172, 177, 178; use of, in determining the exact point of modulation, 79; what to do with it, 171-176.

Music and Poetry, analogy between, 18, 22.
Music and Prose, recitative, 22.
Musical Form (*see* Form).
Musical sentences, or parts of sentences, are made by the alternation of accented and unaccented bars, 38.

Nearly related krys (*see* Key Relationship).
Ninth, chord of the minor (diminished seventh), in enharmonic modulation, 139-143.
No single note can form a motive, 71, 160.
No single chord can define a key, 77, 160.
No single phrase can form a sentence, 26.
Nocturne, by Chopin, as an example of ternary form, 380, 381.
Normal form of sentences consists of eight or sixteen bars, 220, 221.
Normal rhythm, 74 (I.), 221 (*see* Regular Rhythm).
Notes accented and unaccented, 59, 60.

One note common to two chords used as a means of modulation, 156.
Outlines of hymn-tunes to be filled up, 341.
Overlapping of phrases (*see* Irregular Rhythms).
Overlapping of phrases defined, 45.
Overlapping of sentences commoner than that of phrases, 367.
Overlapping sentences and phrases, examples of, 45, 258-261, 331, 367, 382.

Paraphrasing defined, 344; example of, 344.
Period or sentence defined, 24, 74 (II.).
Phantasiestück, by Schumann, as an example of ternary form, 386-391.
Phrase, accented and unaccented, 50; *cadences at end of a*, 74 (III.), 186; full cadence, 26, 29, 35, 43; half cadence, 24, 27, 28, 34, 42, 43, 45; interrupted cadence, 31; plagal half cadence, 30; inverted cadence, 34 (*b*), 42; containing two sections, 51; defined, 27, 74 (III.); feminine ending in a, 28; fore-phrase and after-phrase, 50; importance of harmonic considerations in, 54; not always divisible into sections, 53, 54, 187.
Phrases, no restriction as to the number of phrases composing a sentence, 74 (III.); overlapping of, 45, 258-261.
Phrasing incorrect, examples of, 362-365.
Poetry and music, analogy between, 18, 22.
Poetry and Prose, a foot defined, 21; accent, 19-21; cadence, 19-21; dis-

tinction between, 19, 20; varieties of verse, 21.
Point of modulation, 79, 160.
Polyphonic music, complex rhythms of, 269.
Prelude by Bach as an example of binary form with two subjects, 330.
Prolongation and repetition of cadence (*see* Irregular Rhythms).
Proportion and balance defined, 10.

Quadruple Time, a compound time, 36; often incorrectly barred, examples, 37.
Quintuple Time explained, 300; examples of, 300-302; irregular compound time, 300; use of dotted bars, 301.

Recitative, analogy between music and prose, 22.
Regular or Normal Rhythm defined, 9, 26, 74 (I.), 220, 221; four-bar sentences explained, 30, 184, 197, 313, 319.
I. SENTENCES OF EIGHT BARS, 184; accented and unaccented bars, 185; cadence at end of fore-phrase, 186; cadence to be in accented bar, 185; commencing with incomplete bar, 185; forming a complete composition, example by Schumann, 200; formula for indicating the sub-divisions of sentences, 188; formula for construction of sentences, 207; harmony, anticipation of, 208, 209; harmony of accented bar continued through unaccented bar, 208; how constructed, 184-187; method of composition, 206; models for, 202-205; phrases in, 184; phrases divisible into sections, 187; sections, construction of, 187; usual modulations, 186; various forms of, 189-193; various forms which modulate, 194-199; where to change the harmony, 208.
II. SENTENCES OF TWELVE BARS, 210; containing three phrases, 210; examples of, 210-214; feminine endings in, 211, 212; formulæ, 210-214; in minuets, 215; often are extensions of eight-bar sentences, 215; similarity of phrases in, 211, 212.

III. SENTENCES OF SIXTEEN BARS, 216 ; cadences in, 216-219 ; containing four phrases, 216 ; examples of, 217-219 ; example of extension from eight bars, 218-219 ; formulæ, 216 ; middle cadences in, 217 ; monotony in the cadences to be avoided, 216 ; similarity of eight-bar sentences, 217 ; subdivision of, 216.

Regularity of cadence in dance-music and smaller compositions, 10, 323.

Relationship of keys (*see* Key Relationship).

Remote modulation in short pieces rare, an example of, 310.

Response implies accent, 59.

Responsive phrase, meaning of, 59.

RHYTHM and melody inseparable, 9 ; defined, 9, 23, 24, 74 (I.) ; irregular (*see* Irregular Rhythms) ; reason for prevalence of, two-, four-, and eight-bar, 26 ; regular (*see* Regular Rhythms).

Rhythmic figure, 180, 210.

"Ritmo di tre battute," in Beethoven's Ninth Symphony, explained, 257.

Scale passages—diatonic and chromatic—used as a means of modulation, 157, 158.

Second degree of relationship of keys (*see* Key Relationship).

SECTIONS defined, 51, 74 (IV.) ; cadences at end of, 52, 55, 56, 74 (IV.) ; cadential feeling less decided than in phrases, 55, 74 (IV.) ; construction of, 187 ; divisible into motives, 58 ; how to find the limit of, 51, 52 ; importance of harmonic considerations in, 54.

SENTENCE OR PERIOD, constructed from typical motive, 177, 178 ; constructed from motive of more than two notes, 179, 180 ; containing two phrases, 24, 27-35 ; containing three phrases, 42, 43 ; containing four phrases, 44-47 ; defined, 24, 74 (II.) ; ending with a half-cadence, 47, 74 (II.) ; ending with a modulation, 34, 35, 194-199 ; feminine endings, 28, 74 (II.)

SENTENCE forming a complete composition, 200 ; normal form of, 25, 26, 220,

221 ; number of phrases in a, 74 (III.) ; of four bars, 30, 184, 197, 313, 319 ; of eight bars, 24, 27-29, 184-209 ; of twelve bars, 42, 43, 210-215 ; of sixteen bars, 44-47, 216-219.

SENTENCES, contraction of (*see* Irregular Rhythms) ; extension of (*see* Irregular Rhythms) ; in three-bar rhythm (*see* Irregular Rhythms); in five-bar rhythm (*see* Irregular Rhythms) ; in six-bar rhythm (*see* Irregular Rhythms) ; in seven-bar rhythm (*see* Irregular Rhythms) ; of irregular construction (*see* Irregular Rhythms); of regular construction (*see* Regular Rhythms).

SEPTUPLE TIME, 300 ; explained, 300, 303 ; examples of, 303, 304 ; irregular compound time, 300 ; use of dotted bars, 303.

Sequential repetition of a bar in a phrase, 243.

Seven-bar rhythm (*see* Irregular Rhythms, 262-264).

Seventh minor in enharmonic modulation (*see* Modulation, Means of).

Short pieces in binary form, how to write, (*see* Composition).

Simple binary form (*see* Binary Form).

Simple ternary form (*see* Ternary Form).

Six-bar rhythm (*see* Irregular Rhythms, 230).

Sixteen-bar sentences (*see* Regular Rhythms).

Sixth, chord of the augmented, in enharmonic modulation (*see* Modulation Means of).

SLOW MOVEMENTS as examples of ternary form, from sonatas by Beethoven, 355, 356, 362-369 ; by Mozart, 357 ; by Weber, 374-377 ; from quartett by Haydn, 359-361.

Sonata form developed from the binary form with two subjects, 336.

Sonata by Mozart, Adagio of, as an example of the binary form with two subjects, 333-335.

SONGS as examples of concise binary form, 310, 318-320 ; as examples of extended binary form, 328 ; strophic, 319 ; as examples of ternary form, 392-394.

STROPHIC songs defined, 319 ; example of, 319.

Subdivisions of a musical sentence, 49, 74 (III., IV., V.), 171; of a musical sentence formula, 188.

Subdominant key, care required in modulating to—why, 346.

SUB-MOTIVES, 68.

Syncopation and cross accents, 287.

TABLE of nearly related keys, 94 (*a*); of key in the second degree of relationship, 94 (*b*).

TERNARY FORM, 348; coda defined, 352; codetta defined, 357; defined, 348, 352, 353, 400; difference between binary and ternary form, 350-353; elasticity of this form, 354, 400; found in almost every department of music, 354; its importance, 348; *the episode,* an essential of this form, 350; defined, 350, 400; form of, 352; keys for, and examples of, 352, 356, 358, 360, 375, 380; time sometimes changed for, 398, 399.

I. IN CYCLIC WORKS, (*a*) slow movement from sonata by Beethoven analyzed, 355, 356; episode in key of submediant major, 356; modulations, 356; rhythmic construction, 355; the time explained, 355; (*b*) slow movement from sonata by Mozart analyzed, 357, 358; coda and codetta, 357; episode in key of tonic minor, 358; (*c*) slow movement from quartett by Haydn analyzed, 359-361; episode in key of flat mediant major, 360; (*d*) slow movement from sonata by Beethoven analyzed, 362-373; incorrect phrasing, 362-365; link defined, 368; found in minuets, scherzos, and slow movements, 378; (*e*) slow movement from sonata by Beethoven analyzed, 370-373; coda, 373; link, 372; (*f*) slow movement from sonata by Weber analyzed, 374-378; episode in unusual key, 375.

II. AS AN INDEPENDENT FORM, found in caprices, nocturnes, impromptus, 'morceaux de salon,' etc., 379; (*a*) nocturne by Chopin analyzed, 380, 381; (*b*) impromptu by Schubert analyzed, 382-385; cross accents, 385; link of considerable extent, 385; overlapping of phrases, 383; (*c*) Phantasie-

stück by Schumann analysed, 386-391.

III. IN VOCAL MUSIC, 392; example by Handel analyzed, 392-394; other examples referred to, 394-396; in modern vocal music, 397.

THEMATIC MATERIAL, analysis of, an example by Bach, 325; by Schumann, 312.

THEMES FOR VARIATION, binary form in, 310; example by Haydn, 316.

Thesis and Antethesis, 26.

Thirteenth chord of minor in enharmonic modulation, 151-153.

Three-bar rhythm (*see* Irregular Rhythms).

Three-part song form (ternary form), 348.

TIME, compound, German definition of, 36; elision of a beat in a bar, 299; grouping the notes of duple and quadruple time to produce the effect of triple time, 287; examples, 290-292; grouping the notes of triple time to produce the effect of duple time, 287-289; how to determine whether a bar of four crotchets is to be considered as one bar or two, 329; insertion of a beat in a bar, 295-297; quadruple time a compound time, 36; incorrect barring in, 37; quintuple, 300-302; septuple, 300, 303, 304; unit of measurement in, 329.

Tonality defined, 7.

Tonic minor key and its relationship to its tonic major, 87.

Transient modulation—transition, 77.

TRIADS, chromatic, modulation by (*see* Modulation, Means of); diatonic, modulation by (*see* Modulation, Means of).

Twelve-bar sentences (*see* Regular Rhythms).

Two-bar motives, 70, 71, 72.

Two-, four-, and eight-bar rhythm, reason for the prevalence of, 26.

Two-part song form (binary form), 337.

Typical forms, 401.

Typical motive, 172.

UNACCENTED BAR, elision of, 248-256; interpolation of, 221-247.

Uniformity of rhythm not often maintained for more than sixteen bars—why, 221, 321.

UNISON PASSAGES, implied harmony in, 44 ; modulation by (*see* Modulation, Means of).

Unrelated keys (*see* Key Relationship).

Variety of cadence in composition, importance of, 346.

Variety of verse, 21.

VOCAL MUSIC, binary form in (*see* Binary Form) ; ternary form in (*see* Ternary Form).

Waltz by Schubert as an example of concise binary form, 315.

MUSICAL ILLUSTRATIONS.

ARNE, "Artaxerxes," 26.

BACH, J. S., Cantata, "Ach, ich sehe," 101 ; Cantata, "Ich bin ein guter Hirt," 135 ; Cantata, "O Ewigkeit, du Donnerwort," 138 ; Französische Ouverture, 323 ; Johannes Passion, 134 ; Suite Française, No. 6, 327 ; Toccata in D minor, 64 ; Wohltemperirtes Clavier, Fugue 36, 270 ; Wohltemperirtes Clavier, Prelude 39, 330.

BEETHOVEN, Bagatelles, Op. 33, No. 3, 195 ; Bagatelles, Op. 33, No. 7, 73 ; Concerto in G, Op. 58, 32 ; "Egmont," 266 ; "Marmotte," Op. 52, No. 7, 28 ; Piano Trio, Op. 1, No. 2, 209 ; 'Prometheus," 317 ; Quartett, Op. 18. No. 3, 34 ; Quartett, Op. 59, No. 1, 73 ; Quartett, Op. 74, 76 ; Sonata, Op. 2, No. 1, 53, 62, 212 ; Sonata, Op. 2, No. 2, 244 ; Sonata, Op. 5, No. 1, 292 ; Sonata, Op. 7, 111 ; Sonata, Op. 13, 362 ; Sonata, Op. 14, No. 2, 287 ; Sonata, Op. 22, 208 ; Sonata, Op. 23, 178 ; Sonata, Op. 24, 227 ; Sonata, Op. 26, 32, 143 ; Sonata, Op. 28, 40, 70 ; Sonata, Op. 30, No. 3, 288 ; Sonata, Op. 31, No. 2, 124, 287 ; Sonata, Op. 31, No. 3, 150 ; Sonata, Op. 53, 149 ; Sonata, Op. 78, 210 ; Sonata, Op. 79, 355 ; Sonata, Op. 106, 262 ; Third Symphony, 298 ; Seventh Symphony, 100, 156 ; Ninth Symphony, 257 ; Trio in C minor, Op. 1, No. 3, 179 ; Trio in B flat, Op. 97, 121 ; Variations, Op. 76, 194.

BENNETT, W. S., "Paradise and the Peri," 190.

BERLIOZ, "L'Enfance du Christ," 304.

BOIELDIEU, "La Dame Blanche," 301.

BRAHMS, "Ein Deutsches Requiem,' 123.

CHERUBINI, "Anacreon," 183.

CHOPIN, Nocturne, Op. 37, No. 1, 380; Sonata, Op. 4, 302.

CHORAL, "Liebster Jesu, wir sind hier," 309; "O gesegnetes Regieren," 24; "O Gott, du frommer Gott," 30; "Valet ich will dir geben," 31.

CLEMENTI, Sonata, Op. 36, No. 3, 292.

CORELLI, Sonata, Op. 2, No. 1, 313.

CROTCH, DR., Double Chant, 177.

"DUNDEE," Hymn-tune, 308.

DUSSEK, Sonata in G, Op. 39, No. 1, 259.

DVORÀK, "Stabat Mater," 127, 299.

FARRANT, Anglican Chant, 250.

HANDEL, "Agrippina," 295 ; "Alexander Balus," 328 ; "Berenice," 326 ; "Deborah," 31 ; "Messiah," 141 ; "Orlando," 300 ; "Radamisto," 392 ; "Rodrigo," 293 ; "Susanna," 293.

HAYDN, Overture, "Armida," 35 ; Quartett, Op. 9, No. 2, 231 ; Quartett, Op. 17, No. 5, 187 ; Quartett, Op. 17, No. 6, 43 ; Quartett, Op. 20, No. 1, 254 ; Quartett, Op. 33, No. 5, 267 ; Quartett, Op. 50, No. 6, 197 ; Quartett, Op. 55, No. 1, 242 ; Quartett, Op. 55, No. 3, 44 ; Quartett, Op. 64, No. 1, 189 ; Quartett, Op. 64, No. 4, 321 ; Quartett, Op. 64, No. 5, 359 ; Quartett, Op. 71, No. 1, 267 ; Quartett, Op. 71. No. 3, 229 ; Quartett, Op. 74, No. 2, 228 ; Quartett, Op. 76, No. 2, 196 ; Quartett, Op. 76, No. 3, 285 ; Quartett, Op. 77, No. 1, 279 ; Sonata in C, 230 ; Symphony in C, 27, 211, 316 ; Symphony in D, 34, 265 ; Symphony in F, 35 ; Symphony in G, 29, 56, 67.

HUNGARIAN AIR, 255.

LISZT, "Dante Symphony," 303.

MENDELSSOHN, "Athalie," 137; "Elijah," 132, 136; Fantasia, Op. 16, No. 3, 297; "Lieder ohne Worte," Book I., No. 1, 239; Book II., No. 2, 243; Book II., No. 4, 234; Book III., No. 1, 252; Book III., No. 2, 261; Book V., No. 6, 251; Overture, "Melusina," 218; "St. Paul," 54; Variations in E flat, Op. 82, 138

MOZART, Aria, "Per pietà, non ricercate," 224; Clarinet Quintett, 214, 238; "Cosi fan tutte," 217; "Figaro," 14, 248; "Im Frühlingsanfang," 320; Piano Trio in G, 96; Quartett, No. 23, 232, 264; Quintett in G minor, 140, 161; Sonata in C, 182, 357; Sonata in F, 333; Sonata in B flat (Piano and Violin), 193; Sonata in E minor (Piano and Violin), 192; Sonata in E flat (Piano and Violin), 191; Symphony in C, No. 36, 233; Symphony in D, 45; Symphony in G minor, 283; Symphony, "Jupiter," 120; Twelve Minuets, No. 2, 314.

OLD GERMAN MELODY, 45.
OLD SCOTCH SONG, 255.

PROUT, E., Concertante Duet, Op. 6, 256; Piano Quartett, Op. 18, 246.

SCHUBERT, "Alfonso und Estrella," 198; "Ecossaise," Op. 18, No. 7, 199; Impromptu, Op. 90, No. 2, 382; Impromptu, Op. 142, No. 3, 37; "Lazarus," 164; "Momens Musicals," Op. 94, No. 6, 72; Quartett in A minor, Op. 29, 245; Quintett, Op. 114, 145; "Rosamunde," 147, 158; Sonata in A minor, Op. 42, 159; Sonata in A minor, Op. 164, 157; Sonata in B flat, 122, 126, 163; Sonata in E flat, Op. 122, 240; Symphony in C, No. 7, 125, 148, 281; Trauer-Walzer, Op. 9, No. 2, 315.

SCHUMANN, Bunte-Blätter, Op. 99, No. 1, 311; Carnaval, Op. 9, 295; "Der Abendstern," Op. 79, No. 1, 200; Grillen, Op. 12, No. 4, 299; Intermezzo, Op. 4, No. 3, 152; Papillons, No. 1, 310; Phantasiestück, Op. 12, No. 2, 386; Sonata in G minor, Op. 22, 209; Symphony, No. 2, 260; Trio in F, Op. 80, 65; "Von Schlaraffenland," Op. 79, No. 5, 291.

SPOHR, "Last Judgment," 142; Sonata in A flat, Op. 125, 34.

WAGNER, "Die Meistersinger," 131; "Lohengrin," 47; "Tannhäuser," 46, 55; "Tristan und Isolde," 165, 166.

WEBER, Concertstück, 290; "Kampf und Sieg," 33; "Liebeslied," Op. 54, No. 3, 319; "Oberon," 63; Sonata in C, Op. 24, 73, 268, 289, 374.

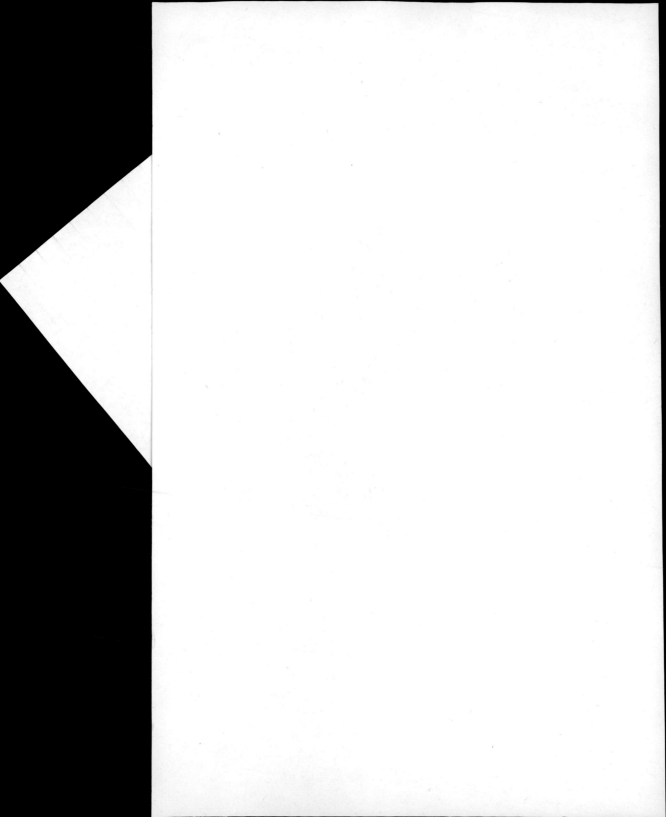

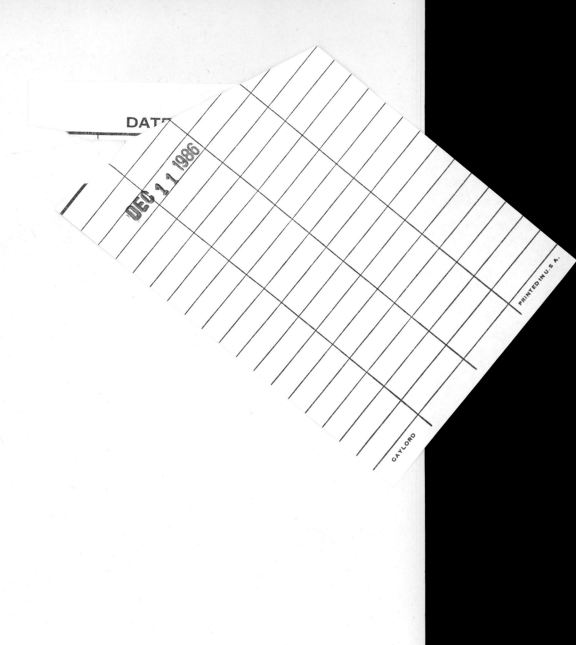